Close More
Sales

Close More Sales

Derrick White

MERCURY

First published in 1992
by Mercury Books
Gold Arrow Publications Limited,
862 Garratt Lane, London SW17 0NB

Set in Concorde by Phoenix Photosetting

Printed and bound in Great Britain by
Bookcraft (Bath) Ltd, Midsomer Norton, Avon

British Library Cataloguing in Publication Data is available

ISBN 1–85251–181–8 (hardcover)
ISBN 1–85252–162–7 (paperback)

CONTENTS

To the West Lothian Majorcans for their eternal good humour.

To the family at Canon Mersey.

INTRODUCTION

You've seen the ads: 'Good Closers Wanted' or worse, 'We Need Closers Not Posers' (or perhaps 'Poseurs' if you read a quality paper). You've heard other salesmen say, often with a degree of reverence, 'He's a brilliant closer'.

It is important to define our terms. Inexperienced salespeople may be misled by the use of 'closing' in the above context. What is worrying about the advertising language is not so much the calibre of salesperson who would apply for the job, but the quality of the company who would choose such terminology. One could forgive someone inexperienced in sales for believing that there was some magic formula or some verbal abracadabra attached to closing the sale. Granted, a poor sales presentation can be redeemed by a good close and a good sales presentation lost by a bad close. All experienced salespeople know the elation of the former and the misery of the latter. However, to imply that closing can stand alone, that there is some cryptic combination of words, like opening a safe, is nonsense.

Sadly, the belief that there might be some arcane system is perpetuated by the very names of closes taught by sales organisations. You'll see them in most books on selling:

The Half Nelson Close
The Reverse Angle Close

1

The Winston Churchill Close
The Puppy Dog Close

These names and others (which we shall be looking at in a later chapter), imply a certain verbal sleight of hand or trickery. Years ago it was not unusual to hear a sales trainer say something like:

> *'You say this.*
> *He says this.*
> *You say this.*
> *And you've got him.'*

The implication was clear. Selling was a form of verbal wrestling. Two good throws, a body slam and bingo! – a submission.

This was not good enough then, it is not acceptable now, and throughout the 1990s it will not even get a look-in.

Recently on Radio 4 a business expert predicted that the number of Europeans seeking business in the UK market this decade 'will be the biggest invasion since 1066'. Clearly the standard of professionalism in a salesperson will be a major factor in this increasingly competitive market place. This book's intention is to examine every aspect of the sales cycle. We shall look at closing as a skill later on. However, let us establish the golden rule now:

You Must Earn the Right to Close

The Allure of the Short Cut
Nothing of value in life is achieved without some effort. The allure of the short cut is very attractive indeed. Slimmers who have struggled with a hundred and one diets still fall for the 'New Diet' or the 'Magic Pill'. They are intellectually convinced that there is no easy way, yet emotionally they hold out hope that perhaps the 'magic potion' exists. It is a very appealing and very old concept. Legends and fairy tales are not complete without it.

The football pools, aphrodisiacs, gensing and a whole

range of 'health' foods, innumerable fitness gadgets, horoscopes, even wrinkle removing creams, are all marketed on the allure of the short cut. Instant results for minimal effort. Language students who have burnt the midnight oil conjugating the verb 'to be' are the first to send off their cheques in response to blandishments such as 'Learn French in Seven Days'. The course soon gets cast aside along with the exercise bikes, wheels, discs and other contraptions which promised the body beautiful.

So it is with closing. If you are selling a fake Rolex in a pub or a set of crockery from a market stall where the price is apparently so ridiculously attractive, then perhaps your entire sale can pivot on the close. (Along with 'Sorry guv-'nor, no cheques, cash only' and 'What do you want a receipt for?')

To sell professionally such items as insurance, home improvements, capital equipment, plant, machinery and other 'big ticket' items, you require a disciplined, structured and convincing sales presentation. There will be several intermediate closes but the culmination of that presentation is The Close. To get there:

You Must Earn the Right to Close.

1

SELLING AS A
PROFESSION

There are several factors which make up the professional salesperson. The greatest is you the individual, and your attitude. A positive attitude to your job is essential.

To the many hundreds of salespeople I have worked with and trained, I often put the question, 'How does the general public view us and our profession?' The answers are usually pretty depressing and include such terms as fast talking, uncaring, flash, lowlife, nuisances, and quite a few others which, with a few exceptions, are wholly unflattering.

I put the question because in any solution-seeking exercise the first step is to understand the problem. Professional salespeople would strongly resent any of the above views; certainly such comments are far less justified than they might have been twenty years ago. However, if such a public perception exists, it is wise to find out why.

Prejudice against salespeople falls under two general categories – valid and invalid. Valid criticism stems from the bad old days when salespeople were often of poor calibre. In the 1950s and 1960s Britain enjoyed an era of full employment. Immigrants even flocked in to take the jobs we were not too keen on and if there was nothing we really fancied at home we could always nip off to Australia for the princely sum of £10. The fare was subsidised by the

Canberra government, so desperate were they to recruit us Poms. As Prime Minister Harold Macmillan told us, we'd 'never had it so good.'

Selling was never a popular occupation and was generally held in low esteem (for reasons we shall look at later). Absurdly, there were even employers who looked upon selling as a necessary evil. Interviews were often cursory. Advertisements regularly concealed the selling role. Training was minimal and instructions like 'Here's your samples, here's your car keys; now go and get some orders' were not uncommon. My favourite was, 'Training? I never had any training. I learned the hard way, son'.

What training there was might consist of learning a set script or spiel. The salesperson's job was to get in front of as many people as possible and recite the spiel. Consequently the salesperson often did come across as 'fast talking' or 'uncaring'. The old-fashioned salesperson did not want dialogue. He feared interruptions and frequently did merit the 'hard-nosed' criticisms to which, unfortunately, we are still sometimes heir. Because of this lack of professionalism in both recruitment and training, much of the public's poor view of salespeople *was* valid.

Happily the situation has improved immeasurably. The people are better and the standards are higher. Alas, there are still enough amateurs in the field to make life difficult for the professional. We can overcome this through polishing the other elements of the pie chart (fig 1 on page 11).

The other form of bias against salespeople is invalid and finds its roots in the old British bogey, class. Prior to the Industrial Revolution everyone knew his or her place. For centuries all power and all wealth lay in the hands of the aristocracy. Then in the eighteenth and nineteenth centuries people began to acquire wealth through making and selling things. We had coal, steel and steam power. We had access to raw materials from an Empire and a captive market in which we could sell our goods. Britain became the workshop of the world.

An unfortunate by-product of this success was that we tended to become a nation of order takers; selling as a skill or as a profession was never seriously considered. Those who followed on – like the Avis Rentacar ads – had to try a little harder. While other nations strove to compete for sales, we became complacent.

Huge fortunes were amassed in the form of 'New Money'. The 'Old Money' closed ranks. Dreadful expressions like *nouveau riche, parvenu* and *arriviste* were employed, the French terms being preferred as a code lest the ill-educated classes might grasp the distaste they implied. Sir Thomas Lipton, a keen yachtsman, founder of the vast chain of grocery shops, found it difficult to find a berth at fashionable Cowes because he was *in trade*.

The sons of the aristocracy, if they were not content to be gentlemen and do no work, could enter the army (preferably a *good* regiment) or perhaps politics. The more aesthetic or less macho sons could enter the Church. With the passage of time the more 'respectable' professions became acceptable. The British Raj in India, however, still referred to those in trade as 'box wallahs'.

An arts degree had more style than a science degree. To this day if you question a cross-section of public schoolboys on their career intentions, their answers are likely to be, 'do something in the City'; 'law'; 'the media'; anything but enter the manufacturing sector. The bias is dwindling but, where it still persists against the manufacturing sector, one can imagine the person who actually *sells* the goods is less than revered.

Because of this absurd, snobbish and quite illogical bias, the sales profession adopted silly names for itself: *Representatives* or *Reps*; *Consultants*; *Advisers* (as in Financial Advisers); *Executives* – anything rather than straightforward Salesmen.

In the United States the historic pattern was the complete reverse. All the US 'aristocrats' – Carnegie, Ford, Rockefeller, Chrysler, Vanderbilt, Getty and so on – made their fortunes making things and selling them. Consequently the attitude in the US towards selling was always more healthy and respectful. Virtually all the books on selling were produced there. British sales managers recommended the works of Dale Carnegie, Frank Bettger, Tom Hopkins, Og Mandino, Zig Zigler and a host of others. These authors were full of homespun idiom such as '*You Wanna Make A Million?*'. The few British books were almost unreadable. Why? Because if we had to write about this beastly business of sales at least we should make the subject as academic or intellectual as possible. Even now there is a ludicrous dichotomy between Sales and Marketing. In the UK, Marketing people may not only dissociate themselves from Sales but actually consider that role somehow beneath them. Their US counterparts see this for the nonsense it is; Sales and Marketing are inextricably linked.

Even the British and American views of success differed. The American was conditioned to believe that everything from a limousine to the US presidency was within his grasp. His British cousin was conditioned to 'know his place'. Symbols of wealth or position merited a touched forelock or envy – a sad relic of a hierarchical, class-ridden society. Success, especially commercial success, was considered rather distasteful, even vulgar. Does any other nation use the phrase 'too clever by half' as an aspersion?

Thankfully, these outdated attitudes are dying. Selling is taking its place where it belongs, in the forefront of commercial skills. We have produced some superb home-grown sales training material, thanks to people like John Cleese and his brilliant Video Arts team, Robin Fielder, Richard Denny, Gavin Kennedy, Sir John Harvey-Jones and a growing list of quality men and women.

In order to get our attitude towards selling right we must feel good about our profession. Any reverence towards the service sector – the arts, the media, banking, law or whatever – is misplaced. Remember, there cannot be a service sector without a sales sector. Unless goods are manufactured and sold, the economy grinds to a halt.

If you are selling a good product or service at a competitive price you can stand tall in any company. Although we call ourselves Salesmen, it is wise to recall the dictum of Robert Louis Stevenson (1850–94): 'Everybody lives by selling something.'

2

PROFESSIONALISM

We have dismissed any invalid criticism based on silly outmoded class bias. Let us now tackle valid criticism relating to a lack of professionalism. An accepted maxim in sales is that you sell four things (in other words, you have four closes):

> yourself
> your product or service
> your company
> your price.

To be truly professional in sales we must address each element thoroughly. For Yourself let's look at the pie chart (fig 1 opposite).

Business knowledge

Picture the situation. The amateur salesman blithely sails into the interview.

'How's business?' he asks.

The businessman looks harassed and complains about the hike in VAT or the UBR or Corporation Tax or some anxiety concerning his day-to-day business. The salesman smiles blankly, completely missing the opportunity to forge a bond of empathy, and attempts to Open The Sale (OTS). His ultimate goal is to Close The Sale but before he can reach the close there are several intermediate closes. One of the earliest closes is YOU, THE INDIVIDUAL. If you work for an exceptional company, have a brilliant product and can offer it at a very low price, then YOU, THE INDIVIDUAL as a close doesn't matter too much. However, life is not like that.

The YOU element is vitally important. People buy from people. They don't just buy from a smart suit or polished visual aids (much as they help), nor do they buy from parrots (hence the failure of the set script or spiel).

It is not necessary to gain a business degree, nor to study

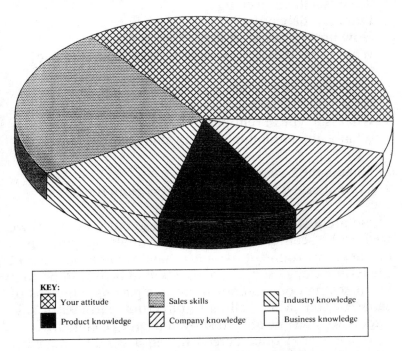

KEY:

⊠ Your attitude   ▦ Sales skills   ◹ Industry knowledge

■ Product knowledge   ▨ Company knowledge   □ Business knowledge

Fig. 1   Make-up of a Professional Salesperson

11

accountancy. But you should have a working knowledge of everyday business terms. See how many of the following questions you can answer:

What is the current rate of VAT?
How often is VAT payable?
To whom is VAT payable?
Is VAT a company liability or a personal liability?
What penalties can be incurred for late or non-
    payment?
What is a profit & loss account?
What is a balance sheet?
What is a cash flow projection?
For whom might a cash flow forecast be prepared?
What is a personal guarantee?
What is a floating charge?
What is a debenture?
How many trading entities can you name?
What is the UBR? How does it differ from rateable
    value?
What are amortization and depreciation?
What is an off-balance sheet lease?
What is a typical rent per sq ft in your city centre?
What is the minimum paid-up share capital for a Ltd
    Co?
What is the base rate today?
At what rate do businesses borrow from the bank?

These are just twenty questions chosen at random. If we wish to be seen as business professionals operating in a business environment, we must have some awareness of the terminology used. Granted it would be less important when selling door-to-door in double glazing, kitchens or cable TV, but when selling to directors, partners or sole traders we must be able to show a degree of empathy.

As a buyer, I once agreed to see a vending machine salesman who was making a cold call. I explained he'd have to be brief as my bookkeeper and I were working on an overdue VAT return. He commented, 'Oh, that time of year again? Musn't keep the Inland Revenue waiting, eh!'

I didn't bother to correct his two glaring mistakes (VAT is paid quarterly to HM Customs and Excise).

Had he shown some understanding of the subject or expressed some interest through asking questions, he might have gained a degree of empathy which could have allowed him more time to progress the sale. Imagine if he had said, 'Is that your March return? You are a wee bit late, and these Customs and Excise people don't mess about nowadays, do they?' Immediately my respect for him would have risen and the beginnings of a rapport would have been kindled.

Certainly, business knowledge does constitute only a small percentage of a professional salesperson's knowledge store but there are occasions where it can help close the gap between buyer and seller. Businessmen appreciate the company of other businessmen, which is one of the reasons why Chambers of Commerce, Rotary and Round Table Clubs exist.

If you sell into the business environment it is wise to keep your finger, even lightly, on the pulse of commerce. Most newspapers have a comprehensive City page. The *Sunday Times* and the *Observer* business sections both give an excellent summary of the week with some well-informed comment. The *Mail on Sunday* has developed an excellent City page which is both informative and unstuffy. Radio and TV also have good, if brief, coverage. Surprisingly, the more you follow the business world, the more interest. City pages sometimes look a little daunting to the new reader but soon the link between 'hard' news and City news becomes apparent.

There are also a number of 'Teach Yourself' books and tapes on business studies. When one considers the number of hours the average salesperson spends in a car, then multiply it by the number of hours he or she spends listening to pop music, the total would equal the amount of time needed to obtain a degree at the Open University. The range of educational audio tapes is now vast.

A Chambers Dictionary definition of professionalism is 'The competence of those who are highly trained and disciplined'. Unless we can lay some claim to this definition we cannot call ourselves professional, and some of the unpleasant criticisms listed in Chapter 1 will be valid. All the other professions – law, medicine, architecture and so on – involve years of study, lectures and immersion into numerous textbooks. For a salesman to expect to enjoy high credibility and high earnings after a few days' training and a few chapters of Dale Carnegie is just not realistic. In any trade or profession the greatest tutor is experience and many experienced sales people earn very substantial incomes. Experience does not come overnight so while it accumulates, don't do it all yourself, learn from others. The fact that you are reading this book shows you have the right attitude.

The twenty-by-one disease

This particular ailment needs a mention. I met quite a number of people in the motor trade who suffered from this dreadful affliction. You can recognise the symptoms by such outward manifestations as, 'I've been selling for twenty years. I don't need any books', or 'After twenty years, I've heard it all,' or 'You can't teach me anything about selling'.

Often what they mean is they have had *one year's experience repeated twenty times.*

One sufferer I knew used to shout across the showroom at some unsuspecting prospect, 'Can I help you?' The intention was to get the prospect before any of his colleagues did and to hold the prospect before he slipped out of the showroom. The effect was pretty predictable. All the prospect's fears of second-hand car salesmen were fulfilled as Big J. bore down on him, nipping his cigarette en route. The exchange normally ended with BJ complaining bitterly about 'another time-waster'. We may not all want to learn from training material, but we should at least learn from experience.

Perhaps part of the problem in the UK is that the standard of retail selling is so poor that the benchmark for sales skills is set far too low. There are some admirable exceptions. Marks & Spencer staff generally seem to have good product knowledge and – equally important – appear to have an element of pride in the company. Alas, it is the exception that proves the rule. Staff in shops, bars and restaurants – especially hotel restaurants – often seem poorly trained and lacking in product knowledge.

We'll look at retail selling in a later chapter.

The next section of the pie chart (fig 1 on page 11) is:

Industry knowledge

This is a double-edged sword. Understand your own industry and the type of industry on which you call. Knowing your own industry allows you to carry out a SWOT (*Strengths; Weaknesses; Opportunities; Threats*) comparison. Whatever you sell – advertising, cars, copiers, furniture, IT, insurance, faxes – it is important to know the opposition. On the odd occasion, aloof ignorance (feigned or real) can be impressive, as in, 'I'm sorry, Mr Buyer, but we are so far ahead I really cannot tell you about Brand X'.

These occasions are rare.

Understanding the industry into which you are selling always impresses the buyer. Experienced salespeople use this very effectively by showing they have a grasp of the problems or *modus operandi* of the industry they are visiting or perhaps by explaining how they have helped companies similar to the buyer's.

Company knowledge

This is also a double-edged sword. Know the strengths of your own company. Equally important, try and do some research on the company you are selling into. I once accompanied a salesman on a call to a firm of architects in Edinburgh. His opening question was; 'What sort of houses do you build?'

A harmless enough opening question to get the conversational ball rolling. Unfortunately, this firm did not build houses. Some cursory research before the call could have established that they specialised in bridges and other major contracts. Many sales manuals refer to the 'REI' of call preparation – *Research, Experience, & Informed Guess*. An informed, intelligent guess as to how your product or service could help a company is useful. More useful is experience, where you have worked with several comparable companies. Best of all, research the company.

A friend of mine sold management consultancy services. His calls were all to blue chip companies with multi-million pound turnovers. The service he sold consisted of a team of financial, productivity and efficiency experts moving into a company to increase profits. Before he made his call, he received from his head office a portfolio on the company. The range of information was considerable – sets of accounts, names of directors, organisational charts, acquisitions, subsidiaries, dates, etc. He made notes and read all the information into a tape recorder so that by rereading the notes and listening to the tape he became thoroughly conversant with all the major aspects of the company, the key people and its *modus operandi*.

At the appointment, the salesman was able to close the 'YOU' and the 'YOUR COMPANY' doors (fig 2) quite quickly

PROFESSIONALISM

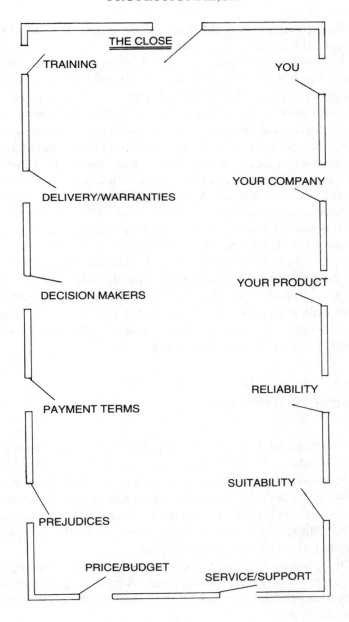

Fig. 2   The Closing Corridor

17

by sheer professionalism through his display of a thorough grasp of the company he was visiting.

This level of research is not necessary in most selling situations, but understanding how powerful a tool it can be will prompt us to carry out that degree of research necessary to make a particular call. For high-value sales and major account sales, good research and good record keeping are essential. Even with detailed research a level of probing is always necessary. With minor sales the ratio of probing to research would change dramatically. Be very careful of assumptions. A company interested in a single typewriter, desk or fax machine may not seem to merit much research. However, it could be expanding or part of a group of companies with a central buying authority.

Incidentally, it is appalling how sadly the research tool is neglected in one of the most important sales calls of all – the job interview. Interviewers are always impressed by applicants who know about the company they seek to join.

Knowing your own company and its strengths is also essential. Let's look at that along with:

Product knowledge

With the advent of technology, the difference between many products is narrowing. Cars, hi-fi, TVs, computers, white goods, brown goods, kitchens – the variations in all of them are becoming indistinguishable to the untutored eye. It is therefore all the more essential that the professional salesperson has a high level of both company knowledge and product knowledge.

This is where real sales skills begin. Two of the strongest challenges in any buyer's mind are, 'Why should I buy your particular product or brand?' and 'Why should I buy from your company?'

Many salespeople see these as hostile questions and

respond defensively. The amateur replies with an ill-considered, half-baked answer such as 'Because it's the best' or 'My company is a very reputable company'. But the damage is done by the defensive tone or the body language – a slight shrug of the shoulders, an uncertain smile or an averting of the eyes for a moment's thought.

The professional does not see the questions as hostile. He sees them for exactly what they are – genuine expressions of both doubt and interest. Every buyer wants to know he has made the correct decision; Buyer's Remorse is a well known syndrome in retail sales. Who has not bought a suit, a coat or some other item only to get home and experience that sinking feeling of having made a bad decision? We all need reassurance. In retail sales there might only be two or three closes in the sale – APPEARANCE, QUALITY AND PRICE. These closes are often made by the buyer himself with little involvement from the sales assistant, but the assistant who can speak with conviction and knowledge of the product can retrieve many sales which hang in the balance. That simple level of professionalism can earn respect, orders and repeat business. Why do we not place more value on our retail shop assistants? M & S shares are the best buy in the retail sector, deservedly so.

In corporate sales, there are often many more closes (see Closing Corridor, fig 2). Does the buyer like and trust you . . . your company . . . your product . . . your after sales service . . . your guarantees? – and so on.

So when the buyer asks, 'Why should I buy your product?', the professional has a golden opportunity to respond without any defensiveness whatever. He can list all the strengths and Unique Selling Points (USPs) of his product. Also, by understanding the company into which he is selling, he can relate all the features of his product as direct benefits to the buyer.

I know nothing about lawnmowers but if I were selling them tomorrow, by five o'clock today I would have half a dozen strong selling points rehearsed to a high degree of fluency. Remember, though, the content of what you say is only half as effective as the conviction with which you say it.

There is a phrase in selling, 'Beware product knowledge'. This is wise advice but needs to be clarified. A friend of mine, Frank, sold Land Rovers and Range Rovers in Scotland. He had a colleague, John, who worked with him. John was a Land Rover enthusiast. His product knowledge was superb. He could talk wheel-bases, differential, torque, BHP and all the technical details for ever. Frank's product knowledge was vastly inferior, yet he was the more successful salesman.

On one memorable occasion Frank sold a Range Rover on a single major buying criterion. Granted there were other criteria, such as price, but the primary one was both simple and powerful. The buyer was quite a short and bumptious man. Frank had enthused on how much he enjoyed the 'commanding driving position' and invited the buyer to sit up in the driver's seat. That was, without doubt, the pivot on which the sale hinged. The 'want' was sparked. All Frank had to do was play a little more on the 'want' and then work on the 'need' element. (We'll look at WANT and NEED more closely in Chapter 3.)

John might have lost the Range Rover sale through being too factual. He could have impressed the buyer with his breadth of knowledge. Facts are impressive but in many sales the *factual* element is not enough. It is important to evoke the *emotional* element to clinch most sales.

The caution 'Beware product knowledge' does not mean don't have any. It means use it effectively. When the young blood in the car showroom asks, 'What size engine is it?', he wants to know how fast it will go. Will he cut a dash at the traffic lights? A graphic description of acceleration can be much more effective than a deep inspection under the bonnet. We'll look at buying criteria in a moment but it is worth stressing now that we do not sell the features of our product, or our company, we sell how they will directly *benefit* the buyer.

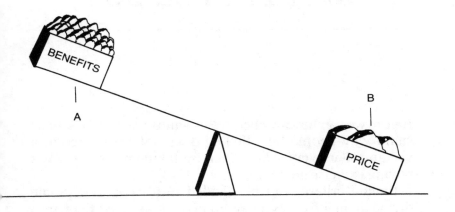

Professional fills 'A'   Amateur empties 'B'

Fig. 3

3

WHY PEOPLE BUY

Before we can be fully effective in selling we have to understand why people buy. Selling does not take place in a vacuum. For every selling exercise taking place there is a buying exercise going on.

Buying criteria can be divided into categories. Some divide them into WANTS and NEEDS. Others split them into DESIRE FOR GAIN and FEAR OF LOSS. The RATIONAL and the EMOTIONAL are yet another two. For corporate sales the criteria are sometimes seen as ORGANISATIONAL NEEDS and PERSONAL NEEDS. All are accurate.

Buying criteria change from person to person and from product to product. Who has not seen someone wearing an article of clothing that you would not be seen dead in; yet someone fancied it enough to spend money on it. The buying criteria for an article of clothing might be as follows:

it keeps you warm
it keeps you decent
it's hard wearing
it's long lasting
it's easily washed/ironed
it's very cheap
it's very fashionable
it looks great.

Any salesperson in the rag trade who tried to sell clothes on the first half-dozen buying criteria would soon starve. If the last criterion – looks great – is really applicable then the others are almost irrelevant, whatever the price. However, if you were selling gardening overalls, clearly the buying criteria would change.

Little or no probing is necessary in the above context. In car sales, more probing is necessary. Just because the young man looks rather yuppie and flash does not mean he wants to look at something sporty. He may have a young family, a dog and a windsurfer and be in the market for an estate car with an integral roof-rack. The pathway to the salesman's grave is paved with assumptions. Do not assume – probe.

Let's look at the various divisions.

Needs and wants

Which is the stronger? Ask any smoker. The smoker will often say, 'I need to get a packet of cigarettes.'

With all the medical evidence available he certainly doesn't NEED them. But people buy what they WANT first. If we only bought what we needed we would all be dressed very similarly in functional, warm and hard-wearing clothes. Colours would be uninteresting and uniform. Cars would all be capable of a maximum of 70 m.p.h. (not only do we not need more, but it is illegal to do more); they would all be adequate to get from A to B and the cost would not exceed £10,000. Few of us would own TVs as only a small minority actually need one. Sales of tobacco, chocolate, sweets, ornaments, perfume and a hundred and one *unnecessary* items would disappear.

The wants-and-needs division is sometimes referred to as POSITIVE PURCHASES and NEGATIVE PURCHASES. Negative ones are rather downbeat – a shoe repair, a new tyre or wing mirror, all a bit of a nuisance and we complain bitterly about the expense. The same man who is furious at paying £15 for a shoe repair will express his displeasure in the pub, buy a round of drinks including the landlord and old Barry in the corner and casually hand over a £20 note, then not even glance at the change. The difference? One was a negative or need purchase. The other was a positive or want purchase.

Cable Television is very much a want sale. The good salesman will firstly probe to establish viewing habits, channels and composition of the household. He will listen carefully for *buying signals* such as 'not enough variety', 'too many repeats', 'nothing on during the day' or any other area of dissatisfaction. Having built a foundation of dissatisfaction he can build his sales case with professionally prepared visual aids and show a whole conucopia of viewing alternatives – sport, entertainment, humour, movies, 24-hour news coverage, in fact a whole range of over thirty channels catering for every taste. However, although the sale is primarily a want sale, the professional will not omit entirely the need element. The children's development can be enhanced with natural history and other more serious programmes. Telephone linkage can provide a better quality line and a saving on calls.

Buying criteria also include less tangible motives such as *being ahead*, *keeping up with the Joneses* or *acquisition*. We are an acquisitive society. (What else could explain the sale of those ghastly ornaments advertised in the colour supplements?) The balance of a cable TV sale could be tipped by an *innocent* remark such as, 'No. 53 across the road has just installed cable.'

So what is the significance of this? How can I be a more effective salesman? Some products may be seen as negative purchases. Take double-glazing. This might be seen in an unexciting need category. The professional salesman will turn it into a want. The quality of the glass, the durability of the surrounds, the expertise of the fitters, the quickness of the installation will not sell the product.

Attractive graphic pictures will. Children running from the bath to the bedroom, all cosy and warm; complete absence of irritating street noise; no huddling up to the fire to keep warm; lower fuel bills to allow more spending on life's little wants – these can turn a negative purchase into a positive one.

Photocopiers may seem a negative purchase: 'Damn nuisance, we need a new one!' The professional should be able to relate as many direct *benefits* as possible to the buyer to turn that need into a want. No maddening trips to the Copyshop during breakdowns; no loss of valuable employee time on such errands; work completed on time; getting home earlier; better image on paper; user friendly; more professional image; saving of time/money/tempers – these generate want.

The amateur seldom thinks beyond the need. The professional establishes the need, proves he can meet the need, then, through stressing benefits, generates the stronger buying motive – the want. Here the importance of closing must be emphasised. Nothing infuriates the salesperson more than having done all the professional selling – generating the want – to find the amateur has nipped in and beaten him purely on price.

Desire for gain and fear of loss

This division is probably the most comprehensive of all. The two factors cover almost every possible human buying motive. Term Insurance is sold exclusively on fear of loss. Endowment Insurance is sold on both fear of loss and desire for gain. Fire extinguishers, security systems, burglar alarms and courier services are sold primarily on fear of loss. Paradoxes can always arise; a millionaire might buy a gun motivated by fear of loss while a thief might buy the same item motivated by desire for gain. Here we return to the basic principle: we must understand why people buy before we can sell.

A fax machine could be sold through both motives. Desire for gain: more professional; more orders; save postage; save telephone time; home earlier through programmed transmissions, and so forth. Fear of loss buying criteria could include: loss of orders; waste of money and time on post; waste of telephone line time through long verbal exchanges.

Desire for gain need not relate to material gain such as greater efficiency and increased economy. It can also include personal factors such as prestige, which relate more to pride and vanity. People who drive Range Rovers in the lowlands of the Home Counties don't buy them just to bring home the groceries from Tesco. The Ferrari owner was not motivated by greater efficiency or economy. Why spend £500 on a leather coat when an anorak would do the same job just as well?

Rational and emotional

The desire for gain and fear of loss division overlaps to a large extent with the similar buying motives of the emotional and the rational categories. Very few products fall completely into one or the other. The professional car salesman knows when to play on the factors of speed, acceleration and flashy looks. He also places emphasis on safety and economy to good effect. In the early days of car telephones the want or emotional element was used strongly. Many buyers couldn't wait to show off by making a call at the traffic lights. Nowadays, the need factor is the main selling point, though the want card is still played, to a greater or lesser degree, depending on the buyer.

Organisational and personal needs

In corporate sales the divisions are often referred to as organisational needs and personal needs. The organisation might need greater efficiency and economy but the skilled salesman also includes the personal benefits. The office manager might wish to look good in the eyes of his or her superiors. A piece of equipment might mean an easier, less stressful life. In some instances the personal need is approached more blatantly – an expensive meal, a ticket to a major sporting event or, to be crass, some form of back-hander. Whatever form it takes, the professional salesman always bears in mind the WIFM factor – (What's In It For Me). You cannot sell on the WIFM factor alone, but it may be the clinching element in a deal which is finely balanced.

Understanding why people buy is the key to successful selling. This is why the old-fashioned spiel or singular line of approach is not good enough. You may hit some of the buying criteria but you may miss homing in on the ones which could be of personal relevance to the buyer.

In the early days of the health club industry in the UK, the 1960s, very few people had heard of one, let alone joined one. It was understood that 'prospects' had reached the peak of decisiveness when they called into the club for details. If they did not join on that day, the peak was passed and the likelihood of a second shot was remote. Consequently the health club sale was recognised as a 'hard sell'; not unethical but extremely thorough.

We learned by heart a series of thirty-six headings, all of which were divided into desire for gain and fear of loss. The questions were very simple but carefully structured so that each one struck a chord with the prospect.

'What weight are you?'

'How long since you were at a healthy bodyweight?'

'What measurement is your waist – hip – thigh, etc?'

'How do you feel after running up a flight of stirs?' (*How does anyone feel!*)

'When did you last do any regular exercise?'

And so on. Question after question. All this came under Section One known as ESTABLISHING THE NEED.

Having completely demoralised the poor prospect on the health aspect, the next step was to concentrate on the vanity element. 'How does your spouse feel about your 40-inch waistline?' You get the picture. Sagging chests, poor posture, self-consciousness in a swimsuit, lacklustre skin, bulging thighs, you name it.

Section Two was the cheerful bit – PROVE YOU CAN MEET THE NEED. First, health: stronger heart, improved circulation, greater stamina and all the benefits of physical fitness. Then came vanity: flat stomach, firm chest, tapered waist, shapely legs – in essence, the healthy body beautiful.

Fluent as the sale had to be, it was far from a scripted spiel. Emphasis could be placed on any area of concern depending on what was established in Section One. For instance, too much stress on the cardiovascular benefits of exercise to a figure-conscious girl would not be as effective as with a middle-aged man. There were many closes en route to the close. Having obtained stage-by-stage agreement on what the prospect wished to achieve, the final Yes on signing the membership agreement was not too difficult to reach.

This, incidentally, is very much history now. Most people are aware of the risks of obesity, lack of exercise or bad diet. Fashion consciousness and the powerful message of the slimming industry have made health club enrolment much easier.

The insurance industry uses a similar approach. Many employ a document known as a 'Fact Find'. Again, a series of questions is asked to establish the need:

'Salary?'

'Children? . . . ages?'

'Dependent relatives?'

'Existing cover?', and so forth.

All this information gathering comes under the heading of PROBING which we'll cover in a later chapter.

This approach to selling is not only logical but universal. Not long ago, I ran a course for a group of business studies students from France. When I came to why people buy, they taught me a useful acronym they use in French commercial teaching. It was S.A.B.O.N.E. or Sécurité, Affection, Bien Être, Orgueil, Nécessité, Economie. In English: Security, Affection, Well-being, Pride, Necessity and Economy. Try to find a product or service which does not come under at least one of these categories.

Just a word on Affection. This could cover gifts and other purchases for loved ones or even a new typewriter for old Mrs Bradshaw who is a simply wonderful employee. It also covers *liking the salesman*. In the motor trade it was not uncommon to find a buyer who could have got the same deal, or better, from a garage down the road. When asked why he chose one and not the other (after all the paperwork had been done, of course), the reply was quite often, 'I didn't like the guy down the road.'

'But it was cheaper there,' we would say.

'I don't care. I didn't like the other guy's manner. I just didn't feel happy.'

How often have you walked out of a shop of a situation where you were prepared to buy, but you did not like the attitude of the sales staff. In some shops it might be more effective to leave an 'honesty box', allowing shoppers to browse and close themselves. Of all the reasons why people buy, the first close is YOU.

4

PROSPECTING

You feel good about your profession. You have a reasonable store of business knowledge. Your product knowledge is first-class. You can make a convincing delivery on the strengths of your company and you understand both your own industry and the industry or consumer field into which you are selling. Let's go and find some prospects.

Every human being is a prospect for some product or service. Efficient time and territory management is all about finding suitable prospects for your goods or service.

In insurance sales, or financial services as we now call it, virtually everyone is a prospect. In cable TV sales it is more specific. Wherever cable is being laid, those streets become part of the prospect bank. Kitchens, double-glazing and water purifiers relate mainly to the domestic market. With office furniture or equipment, all businesses have the potential need for desks, copiers, typewriters, computers, faxes or stationery.

Let's look at the main avenues available for successful prospecting:

cold calling
referrals
social clubs
business clubs and organisations

30

exhibitions
mailshots
telephone sales

Cold calling

In many fields of sales this will always have to be part of the job. There is no substitute for it. Calling on the high street or industrial estates gives you that essential feel for your patch. You can see the type of business, the size, the number of employees, the existing supplier or equipment, businesses opening up or closing down, and a whole wealth of information which no reference book or directory can provide. Most important, it gives you the opportunity to meet people.

Every call should have an objective. Here are three useful categories: *like to get – expect to get – must get.*

A vending machine salesman, for example, would *like to* find a business with soiled coffee mugs everywhere, a kettle standing on a stained tea-towel surrounded by unsightly milk bottles and congealed sugar granules. He would like to meet the appropriate decision-maker and make a brilliant presentation on all the benefits of a clean, professional-looking, economic and labour-saving vending machine. He would also like to enthuse the buyer with both organisational needs and personal needs to the point where he can leave with a signed order.

However, he is a realist. Although he knows the *like* is always possible, he *expects* to talk to a decision influencer, gain some useful information and earn the right to make a future approach call. Failing that, he *must get* a name, a compliments slip and an overview of the existing equipment or lack of it. He may also wish to leave a business card or some pre-prepared literature addressed to the appropriate person. Although necessary in prospecting, the like

31

to get – expect to get – must get formula is the basis for the principles of negotiation, whether it be a pay rise or nuclear disarmament talks. It is surprising how many employees storm into a management office demanding some improvement in pay or conditions without a clear, structured negotiation plan.

It is also surprising how many salespeople have no clear objective on a call. Moreover, it never ceases to amaze me how many salespeople invite the very response we fear most – rejection. Having been both a salesman and a buyer, I treasure the memory of when a young salesman (in fairness, he was more a canvasser employed to play the numbers game) called into my training consultancy in Glasgow. He knocked on our door:

'Excuse me, I don't suppose you're in the market for a photocopier?'

'Not at the moment.' We were courteous enough.

'Okay. Thank you,' he said politely and left.

My partner and I looked at each other in disbelief. How could any employer leave a lad so ill-equipped to wander the commercial world? Ironically, we *were* in the market for a copier and it wasn't long (it never is) before another salesman called. He was a big, smart, friendly chap with a positive manner and good eye contact.

'Forgive me asking,' he said, 'but I notice you don't seem to have a photocopier. How do you make copies?'

We explained our need was not great but we used a printing service when necessary. He asked a few more intelligent, probing questions and began to quantify the need. Then he paused.

'Do you mind me asking – what is it you do here?'

My partner and I exchanged quick, mischievous glances. I replied, deadpan, 'We teach people to sell.'

The salesman blinked, looked at both of us, then with a broad smile said, 'How am I doing?'

You guessed it. We bought a copier from him. A perfect example of liking the salesman or closing the *you* door. I don't think I ever did know the make of the copier; so company and product knowledge (on that occasion) did not enter the equation. The employer of the first 'salesman' not only does himself a disservice, but he also makes life harder for all the rest of our profession. Naturally, any employer wants to play the numbers game for as little expenditure as possible. But quantity is not the only answer. Paying a better quality person to make better quality calls is more effective. Quality people means different things to different sales managers. The old-fashioned always sought 'ambitious, hard working self-starters, eager to make Big Money' or that type of thing. Of course it would be foolish to disregard such qualities. They are valuable for success, but one of the simplest interview questions is, 'Is he or she a likeable person?' or Would I buy from this person?'

A common acronym in sales is MAN, or the person with the Money, Authority and Need. Many old-school managers would instruct salespeople not to bother with office girls, middle-managers and other 'time-wasters' – 'get in front of the MAN.' This is a dangerous over-simplication. It implies a single person whose judgement is absolute. This is seldom the case.

Forget MAN. Better is the abbreviation DMU – the Decision Making Unit. In a small sole proprietor business the DMU is often the singular MAN. However, anyone with major accounts experience will know that the DMU can range from one or two key people to an entire committee or board of directors. Also, the key person in the DMU may actually have no signing authority. For example, the key element of the DMU in a typewriter sale is almost certainly going to be the user. The DMU in a photocopier sale might comprise the secretarial staff, the office manager, the financial director and even the MD.

In domestic sales the DMU is normally the husband and wife together. Kitchen and window salespeople consequently make evening calls. There is nothing wrong with a daytime call to influence part of the DMU but if you want to close the sale you'll need a second visit. The same can apply to financial service sales. Car sales, furniture sales and other big ticket domestic items do more business at weekends when families are together.

Intelligent understanding of each member of the DMU's needs is vital. In office equipment sales, the secretarial staff want to hear about simplicity of use: easily changeable cassettes, ribbons, correction tape; no messy fingers; and other personal needs. The office manager needs more emphasis on organisational needs with some personal: work finished on time; efficient service engineers; reliability; customer training; speed and so forth. He also wants to know he is making the correct recommendation. Here, the salesman must close the product knowledge and company knowledge doors firmly. The buyer is mainly concerned with increased productivity and economy but some personal element, such as improved company image, is useful.

It is perhaps a relic of the 'only speak to the MAN' instruction that some salesmen are still rather cheeky to the lady at reception. Not only might she constitute part of the Decision Making Unit, she might be the boss.

Receptionists and secretaries cannot generally be bothered to tell off a salesman who is on the cheeky side. What can happen is that after the salesman leaves an interview with the buyer, the lady may ask the buyer, 'Are you going to do business with him?'

'I might. Why?'

'He was a right creep.'

All the good work done on a sales interview could be undone through a simple lack of professionalism at reception. The converse is also true. A comment from a key member of staff like, 'He was really nice', could contribute to gaining a sale.

Referrals

A well-known maxim is, 'The best source of referral is from satisfied customers'. Not true.

Certainly they are a good source of referrals but anyone can give you a referral, including those you have failed to sell to. For example, you have been through the sales cycle professionally and perhaps lost the sale in a quotation contest. Your relationship with the buyer is still amicable and businesslike. There is nothing to stop you thanking the buyer for his time and the opportunity to quote, then add: 'Speaking of time, we are reluctant to waste busy professional people's time. Would you know of anyone who might be in the market for—?' If the answer is 'No', try a prompt or two. 'Perhaps a business you deal with, or a colleague?' etc.

Providing your relationship is good, a non-buyer is as likely to give you a referral as someone who has bought.

No industry places more emphasis on referrals than the insurance industry. Some companies expect as many as eight referrals with each sale. Their method is both clever and simple. The question is asked, 'Who else in the family or circle of friends or business colleagues might be interested in—?'

Get the names and/or relationships first. 'Well, there's my brother . . . perhaps my assistant manager . . . a girl in my office is looking for a mortgage.'

'Anyone else?'

The logic is not to interrupt the flow by stopping for full names, addresses and phone numbers. All that can be added later. Some insurance organisations will not credit the salesperson with the sale (for league table and recognition purposes) if he or she fails to produce the requisite number of referrals.

There are also Hidden or Unintentional Referrals, as in, 'The machine we have is useless.'

The professional salesman never crows by replying, 'Typical Brand X'. He says, 'I'm sorry to hear that. That brand has quite a good name in the industry.'

When you offer a token defence for the product, the user will often defend his corner even more strongly. 'Good name? I can tell you it's a load of rubbish. And I'm not the only one. The factory unit across the road has one and they have the same problems.'

You get two results. You've increased his desire to change his product, and you've got a referral.

Social clubs and business clubs & organisations

These really belong under referrals. It goes without saying that you will not be popular at the squash club or Round Table meeting if you go round the members trying to sell insurance or measure them up for a suit. However, you can be businesslike and retain your dignity (and possibly your membership) simply by letting people know what you do.

Having exchanged pleasantries with other members there is nothing wrong in adding, 'I come here to relax. I never mix business with pleasure but just so as you know, I'm an estate agent. If I can be of any assistance to you or anyone you know, please let me know.'

Thus, you can become known as Ernie the estate agent, or Colin the computer specialist, or Harry the hit-man for that matter. Members of clubs and other groups often need not go outside their own group to find a specialist in something. Do make yourself known. You'll also see business cards of members on many club noticeboards.

The only exception to the 'make yourself known' rule I can think of was a doctor who joined my gym. The last thing he wanted was being presented with various parts of other members' anatomy in the sauna, when all he wanted to do was rest.

Whenever I leave a Chamber of Commerce or Rotary Club meeting I seldom come away without half a dozen business cards. This makes any follow-up on the telephone so much easier. The dreaded question, 'What's it in connection with?' is comfortably handled with a reference to the Chamber or Rotary meeting. (We'll look at telesales in a moment.)

Exhibitions

These can provide an excellent source of prospects, with company after company represented at stand after stand. A salesman can collect a polythene bag full of literature, contact names and business cards. Generally, stands are manned by other salesmen only too happy to talk to any interested party. If your product or service is somehow linked to the company whose stand you stop at, not only can you obtain a contact name but you can also leave a business card and ask your opposite number to give it to the appropriate person. Keep the stand salesman's card as this will make the telesales call easier. It is worth stressing that with many telephone calls the most difficult task is in getting through to the correct person. So any link, be it Chamber of Commerce, Round Table, the Masons even, or exhibitions, is always useful.

When attending exhibitions take plenty of business cards with you. A colleague and I went to a huge exhibition at the Barbican recently. We stopped at many stands and spoke with many people. We collected a business card at every stop we made. The staggering thing was how few stand staff asked us for a business card. When you consider the time, effort and cost involved in planning and setting up a stand, often for only a couple of days, it defies belief how slack exhibitors can be in obtaining contact names and addresses. Many 'salesmen' simply hand out brochures. So if you publicly exhibit your product or service at a stand, you can be either active or passive. If you choose to be passive, you are wasting the money spent on the exhibition (which nowadays is very substantial). Be active. Plan. Decide what you are going to say in advance. Prepare a visitors' book and plan how to invite people to fill it in. Collect business cards always with the question, 'Who would be the person who would make decisions on—?'

It is not uncommon to hear exhibitors say, 'We spent a fortune on an exhibition and it was a waste of time.' The truly honest must ask themselves, 'Whose fault was that?'

The other string to the exhibition bow is where you hold a form of open day at your own factory, showroom or premises. The principles are exactly the same. This is a job for what I call 'Kipling's Six'. You probably know the rhyme:

> I had six honest serving men
> They taught me all I knew
> Their names were What and Why and When
> And How and Where and Who.

Each of the following questions has to be brainstormed thoroughly and then planned for in detail.

(a) Why am I having the exhibition? What is my objective? Is it just a PR exercise? Are we after orders? Are we after leads with names and addresses?

(b) Who shall we invite? Why? How shall we invite them? Mailshot? Telephone call? Mailshot *and* telephone call? Which members of staff should attend? Duties of each? (I recall an office equipment exhibition where nobody told the receptionist.)

(c) What products shall we display and why? Layout and support material. Whose responsibility?

(d) When to have the exhibition/open day. Advantages and disadvantages of eg a Monday? A Friday? Does it conflict or coincide with another event? Support advertising?

(e) Where? Is existing venue interesting or accessible enough? Would a hotel or exhibition centre be more effective? What about somewhere really original?

(f) How? The *How* factor could be used for emergency provisions, as in, *How will we cope if*. . .? Here a brainstorm of every eventuality could be carried out. Provision could then be made for absent staff, mechanical breakdown, too many enquiries at one time or whatever circumstance might affect your exhibition.

Point (b) above may seem simple enough. But even deciding to promote an exhibition through mailshot and follow-up telephone call is only the beginning. The mailshot must be planned (we'll look at that next), as must the telephone follow-up. I've heard follow-up calls which sounded downright confrontational. 'Could I ask you why you are not coming?' . . . 'Why can't you make it?'

On the other hand I overheard a girl with a wonderful friendly voice. When an invitee said he could not attend she replied, 'Oh what a pity. It'll be a super day. I'm sure you'll enjoy it. Do try and make it.'

That level of attractive charm gets results.

Mailshots

This is a sales medium I have worked with over many years. I have collected a large file labelled 'Mailshots – The Good, The Bad & The Bloody Awful'. There are long ones, short ones, colourful ones, dull ones, funny ones, some full of impact and some with none at all.

A little background is necessary. When the mailshot medium was first used, they were relatively rare and most of them got read by the recipients. Mailshots constituted only a very small percentage of commercial and domestic mail. People were quite intrigued to receive a letter addressed to them. Looking back it is interesting to see just how long some of these earlier sales letters were: paragraph after paragraph about the product or service and why one should buy it.

The response rate was high, up to 10 per cent in some cases. Naturally the companies involved were delighted and so the volume increased; but as the volume increased so the public became inured to them and the response percentage decreased. New tactics had to be devised. Letters were marked *Urgent,* or *Confidential,* or *Your prize draw number is inside* or the rather naïve *Do not throw away, this is not a circular.* The other device is to make the mailshot look as personal as possible, sometimes by inserting your name in several blanks throughout the text of the letter often with hilarious results, as in:

> *Dear Mr White,*
> *This is to tell you Mr White, that your name –*
> *D. White – has been entered in our prize draw . . .*

Visually it looks very smart but it reads appallingly.

More than half the mail now received in a business can be considered mailshots (also known alas as 'junk mail'). Surprisingly, research shows that most of it is looked at. Not necessarily read, but looked at. Why? Well, think of those glossy inserts which tumble out of every magazine and colour supplement, usually as you are leaving the newsagent. You want to kick them into the gutter but being a responsible citizen you pick them up. Having picked them up you glance through them, just in case there is some really special offer that appeals to you. So with the mailshot. Open-minded business people and buyers always like to keep alert to goods and services which may benefit them. Also they often simply look for good ideas as marketing tools for themselves. They are often quite impressed just by creative and professional presentation. One of the best mailshots I have seen was for a cattle worming product.

The insert had a cow's head. When taken from the envelope two elasticised panels shot out from the side, giving the cow handsomely extended horns. It looked brilliant. Sadly, I had no use for the product, but it was a first-class mailshot.

Knowing that most people who look at mailings do so only for a few seconds before consigning each one to the wastepaper bin, the following rules for a mailshot make sense:

1 Must be visually appealing.
2 Must follow A.I.D.A.
3 Must have good heading and postscript (PS) or none at all.
4 Must pass the 'So what?' test.
5 Must pass the W.I.F.M. test (What's in it for Me?).
6 Must be 'You' oriented, not 'I'.
7 Avoid old-fashioned 'waffle-speak'.
8 Always re-read it as the recipient, and remember 5-second rule.
9 Use Targeted Mailshots instead of Blanket Mailshots.
10 Avoid negatives, e.g. 'In the event of breakdown'.
11 Keep the format but regularly change the vein.
12 Don't lead with the chin.

Much of the above is self-explanatory but some amplification is necessary. Firstly, the mailshot must look good. Time and effort spent on it is well spent. For goodness' sake don't waste that effort with badly typed envelopes, misspelt or inaccurate names, bad copies, printing errors, names in the letter which do not correspond to the ones on the envelope (it happens), grey paper, long or no paragraphs, squashed typescript, or anything which detracts from the attractiveness or professionalism of your mailshot.

A.I.D.A. (Rule 2) is probably the oldest acronym in marketing. It is also the best and will never change. The first requirement in any advertisement is to grab the ATTEN-TION. Having gained ATTENTION, we must hold the INTEREST. Then the punch: generate some DESIRE for your product or service. Now you want some form of ACTION.

The perfect mailshot came through my letterbox recently. In extra bold letters on one side it read,

Is Your Bottom Dirty?

Would it grab your attention? It certainly did mine. It also achieved the next essential, it held my interest when it briefly listed the dangers of salt and dirt to the underside of my car. It then generated desire by telling me that a Super New Car Wash service had opened on my block. Action was simplicity itself: just take along the leaflet and I could claim a half-price car wash. To assist the action, a neat little map was drawn at the foot of the page. A.I.D.A. to absolute perfection. Also very inexpensively produced – unlike the cow's horns which, though beautifully produced, must have cost a fortune in both design and production costs.

Another one was a sheet of thin card with circular holes, a perfect replica of a cylinder head gasket. It had a simple label tied to it reading, 'You'll probably blow your gasket when you find out how much you are paying for . . .' Attention and interest straight away. Desire was a challenge to see their 'unbeatable' price list. Action was to return the label with name and address.

We all have a natural grasp of good verbal communication skills. How often do we hail a friend with, 'Hey Fred! Guess what?' You instinctively grab his attention and hold his interest. If you followed with, 'Oh, forget it. It doesn't matter,' Fred would never forgive you. We have the inherent ability to capture our audience in speech, yet somehow we lose it when we write a letter, even a sales letter.

'Dear Sir or Madam' is hardly going to send a frisson of excitement through the reader. Having completely failed to grab any attention it goes on, 'Allow me to introduce myself. My name is A.N. Other and I work for ABC Ltd. We supply . . .' Riveting stuff. You can hardly tear your eyes from the page. *Me . . . myself . . . my name . . . I . . . we . . .* But remember Rule 6: Must be 'You' oriented, not 'I'.

Rule 4: Must pass the 'So what?' test, and rules 5 and 8: Must pass the W.I.F.M. test, and Always re-read as the recipient and remember the 5-second rule. The five seconds are what it takes for the reader to scan the mailshot and establish if the contents are of any interest. If you begin letters with 'allow me' or 'may I' or really go to town and lead with the chin (as in one recent howler: 'It is possible you may never have heard of my company, but . . .'), you'll use up those seconds before you obtain any attention or interest.

Perhaps the old British bogey of class or snobbery alluded to in Chapter 1 intrudes here. Speech can be a bit sloppy but letters, they really should be *nice* or *proper*. Certainly in business correspondence, language should be correct and attention paid to good syntax, semantics and punctuation. Legal letters and any communication which might form part of a contractual exchange have to be very precise indeed.

This need not apply in a mailshot. The whole ethos of a mailshot is effective communication. The essence of good communication is clarity and brevity. The question to ask is not, 'Would it pass muster with my old English master or in Fowler's *English Usage*?' but 'Will it help sell my product or service?' (There are occasions when 'Yes' would be desirable to both questions, as in promoting a legal practice or accountancy service.)

But unless the nature of your goods or service merits a slightly more formal approach, the objective of a mailshot is impact. Cartoons, colour, challenging statements, questions, freebies, pop-up pencil holders or novelties of any kind all contribute to the first two essentials – attention and interest.

Many guidelines on mailshots insist that a heading and a PS should always be used. Consequently you will see mailshots with a heading that completely lacks impact and PSs which range from dull to downright silly. The PS is the written equivalent of verbally calling somebody back into a room. If someone were leaving a room and you called him back to say, 'It's a nice day', you would be considered at best, odd.

Similarly with a PS: unless it has impact, leave it out.

The reason why the PS is considered a must in most training literature is because in test after test it has been proven that people always read the PS, even in a long letter where they skip chunks of the text.

Rule 3: Must have a good heading and PS or none at all. If we work on the principle that we only have five seconds to grab the reader's attention, we can appreciate the importance of a strong heading. A friend of mine is a professional motivational speaker. He uses a mailshot on which the edges of the paper are slightly burnt. Bits of black scorched paper fall off the letter when opened. His heading reads, 'This News is so Hot, the Paper can catch Fire.' Would you read on? Of course you would.

Another one of his was to screw up the letter and post it in a little box. When smoothed out the letter read, 'Just in case you are not excited by this news, I've screwed the letter up for you.'

An attractive use of humour and a good attention grabber. However, it does risk breaking Rule 12: 'Don't lead with the chin.' Salespeople endure enough rejection in life without unnecessarily inviting more.

Really effective headings and mailshot content take time. One of the best ways of achieving good quality and impact is to brainstorm it. Preferably in a group, just throw ideas at a flip chart or sheet of paper. Remember the golden rule of a brainstorm – nothing is rejected or wrong. Rejecting or being scornful of people's ideas only inhibits them from making further contributions. The object in a brainstorm is to plaster as much information or as many ideas as possible onto paper. Afterwards you have all the time you need to prioritise, delete, reject or utilise the concepts you choose.

An excellent mailshot was produced by an office equipment sales team. Firstly, they chose several targets. One was solicitors. Next they brainstormed every legal term they could think of. The flip chart was spattered with little puns such as, 'You be the Judge and Jury' and words like *bench, lease, brief, advocate, evidence* and so on. Then they put together a first-class shot on the theme of the importance of crystal clear, easily read documentation. But the icing on the cake was the heading which read, 'If it's illegible, is it illegal?'

The result was that in every follow-up phone call where the salesman reached the solicitor to whom it was addressed, the solicitor in question remembered reading the letter. One even asked the salesman, 'What exactly did you mean – If it's illegible, is it illegal?' Mission accomplished. Attention held and interest generated, in just six words.

An organisation which provided a conference support service targeted a mailshot to hotels and conference centres. The heading on the letter was as strong as it was brave: 'Are you equipped for modern conferences?' A tiny bit confrontational but the vast majority of conference facility managers would read on, if only to check they were not being left behind.

Another useful attention grabber is to take a headline from a newspaper which is pertinent to the industry you choose to mail. If you provide a training service, there are daily items in the papers bemoaning the lack of training in the UK and its necessity if we are to compete in the European Community. In the health club industry we used newspaper items on the benefits of exercise to health, efficiency and reduction of absenteeism. We enclosed the copy along with a mailshot for corporate memberships. Our heading would be something like, 'How many man hours does sickness cost you?' or 'Is absenteeism a problem in your company?'

Don't be afraid of a bit of confrontation. Better to have a lively, even slightly contentious letter which gets read than one of the dreary old-style, 'Allow us to introduce ourselves. Our company was established . . .' All very polite and nice, possibly with graceful syntax and punctuation-perfect. But it needs more 'You' and less 'I'. At the risk of being impertinent, try saying to a series of women, 'I can show you how to achieve a beautiful body.' Then try saying, 'I've got a beautiful body.' Not much doubt about which would evoke the greater interest.

Remember too, the finest A-level prose is quite literally useless if no one reads it.

The advertising industry has never been afraid of being contentious or provocative. Frequently the TV advert with the highest irritant factor promotes a product which becomes a best-seller. Remember the anti-fur industry advert with its theme of *Rich bitch – Dead bitch*. The accompanying controversy gave the advertisers more prominence than their adverts.

My favourite mailshot heading came from a lady in Birmingham who sold computer software and word-processing systems. Her letter began

'I wandered lonely as a cloud'
(*How much are your Words worth?*)

So far the emphasis has been placed on the first two letters of A.I.D.A. – Attention and Interest. The remaining two, Desire and Action, are equally important. However, A & I have to be superior in importance simply because if they are not achieved then D & A become irrelevant.

You have grabbed the attention and held the interest. Your next task is to generate some desire. Here interest and desire can overlap. Whatever your product or service, you have to thrust home the benefits of it to your reader. A lawnmower mailshot might include a picture of a perfectly manicured lawn with a smug and satisfied gardener dozing in a deckchair. It could list a collection of user benefits; quicker, a delight to use, safe and any of a host of others from the categories covered in Chapter 3 – Why People Buy.

Whatever your product or service, only you can know how to convey the benefits of it. However, do be brief and clear. Do not make the mistake of talking 'features'. The GL car with a 16-valve engine is one thing. Cruising silently at 70 m.p.h listening to a concert in perfect stereo is quite another.

Action can take several forms. You can conclude with lines of unspeakable drivel like 'If you have any further queries in this matter, do not hesitate to contact the writer in the first instance. Assuring you of our best attention at all times. I remain, Sir, your obedient servant, etc.'

God knows who first penned such verbal garbage but somehow it has found its way into thousands of word-processors throughout the country. No human being would dream of speaking such pointless waffle. Why on earth do people write it? Apart from it being waffle it is also semantic nonsense. 'If you have any *further* queries . . .' The recipient has not had any queries so far, so why the 'further'?

If the essence of a good mailer is clarity and brevity, why clog it up with padding? Also avoid all those hackneyed truisms: 'Many businesses today are finding it difficult . . .' and so on. Okay, there is a touch of You and W.I.F.M. here but it is so tortuously laboured you can hear the reader say sarcastically as he screws it up, 'Tell me about it!'

The simplest form of action is where it is left with the sender: 'I will call you in a few days to see how my company might of be assistance to you'.

You can enclose a business card and ask the recipient to call you if you wish, but your response will be negligible (unless the desire element of your mailer is really something).

You can enclose a reply paid card with boxes to tick for

further information. You'll get a better response from this. Survey questionnaires can be very successful if well designed. Clear single-line questions with large clean boxes to tick or fill in somehow attract people. Innocent looking headings like 'We Need Your Help' do get results.

One reason why mailshots regularly end, 'If you have any queries, do not . . . etc.' is because it is easier. The onus is placed on the recipient. You have done your bit. You can sit back now and hope some replies come in. Successful people *make* things happen.

Just a few general points. Rule 10 – Avoid negatives. There is an excellent phrase common in the United States. 'If it ain't broke, don't fix it.' In the motor trade salesmen were discouraged from talking about the down side of motoring such as breakdowns, punctures etc. Even the phrase 'trouble-free motoring' was frowned upon just because of the word 'trouble' – despite its hyphenation.

My Glasgow office received a mailer from a facsimile distributor. It was one solid block of unattractive text. No heading. No PS. When it finally got to the point about fax machines, the letter went on at some length about its service engineers, how they were all over the country and would get to us the same day as the breakdown. The engineers were highly trained and they carried lots of spares. The mailer offered discounts (why?) on service agreements. The image created was one of abject misery. Faults; breakdowns; call-out times; spare parts. Not one benefit of the desire for gain category was listed. Nothing about instant communication; pages of information from and to the rest of the world in seconds; vast economy in telephone line time, and so forth.

Granted, you cannot avoid the downbeat side of a product or service, especially mechanical products. But if you have to refer to the downbeat, at least concentrate on the upbeat first. If you were selling a skiing holiday you would not begin by stressing how competent the ambulance and medical services are when the holiday-maker breaks a leg.

Mailshot – Blanket or Trickle?

Salespeople generally prefer the blanket mailshot. A mailing list can be bought or made up using appropriate directories. The addresses can run into thousands. Because of the sheer volume, the shot remains impersonally addressed to the Managing Director, the Senior Partner, the Headmaster, the householder or whatever designation is appropriate. The letters begin, 'Dear Sir or Madam', 'Dear Proprietor' or with some equally lifeless salutation. We have acquired 'Dear Friend' from across the Atlantic which is no better than the others. All invite a high percentage of rejection. However, the object is volume and a good blanket mailshot can achieve responses in the order of one per cent, sometimes more in a well-presented and well-directed mailer.

Some bought listings will include a name, which will normally render the mailer more effective. Unfortunately, experience shows that many of these listings are out of date. If the addressee left the company, or even died, some two or three years previously, reactions can range from the disdainful to the hostile.

The reasons blanket shots are preferred are simple: high volume achieved and effort may be minimal. Some mailing services will undertake the entire task. All the salespeole have to do is sit back and wait for a response.

The successful make things happen. That is why the trickle mailshot is more effective.

The formula is *Call – Send – Call.*

First choose your target, then telephone. 'Good morning. I wonder could you help me please? To whom should a letter be addressed regarding—? Is it the senior partner or is there a specially nominated person?'

This is a very good opening. The reason some receptionists are so defensive is usually because the employer has given firm instructions not to put sales calls through. By asking for help, then for the appropriate addressee for a letter, you relax the person we sometimes call 'the gate-keeper'. You'll normally get the name. Check his or her title. Check the address and postcode, then thank the receptionist.

'You've been most helpful, thank you, what's your name? . . . Thanks Susan. My name's John Smith. I'll be writing to Mr Jones and I'll call him in a few days to discuss the letter.'

This type of shot is known as Trickle because you only do so many every day, perhaps twenty. It is not difficult to obtain twenty names in this way. Then send off your mailer, written specifically for the industry or profession you have chosen. The follow-up telephone call – three days later – is much easier. 'Good morning. Is that Susan? Hi, it's John Smith. I wrote to Mr Jones on Monday; could you put me through, please?' Of course, this is no guarantee to being connected but the success rate is much higher than a cold call or if you were following up a blanket mailshot.

The Trickle, call – send – call, takes a little more effort but the results are much greater. The first call can be made either on the telephone or cold canvassing. Another benefit of the Trickle is that it gives the salesperson a structure. If you sent out just ten mailers on a trickle basis every day – great, because every day you also have ten warmish follow-up calls to make. In relaxing the receptionist by just asking for help, you have the opportunity to establish a rapport which can mean that her role as gatekeeper can be less obstructive.

Whenever you hear the dismissive comment, 'Mailshots don't work', the first factor to question is not medium. The medium is as good or as bad as you make it. Question the message.

Telephone sales

As with the cold calling – and for that matter any element of the sales cycle – an OBJECTIVE is essential. With some telesales calls, such as stationery and other consumables or classified advertising, the objective will probably be to sell on the telephone. With other bigger ticket items such as display advertising, insurance, plant, machinery or office equipment, the objective will be to sell the appointment. Once you have a clear objective you can plan towards it.

The professional is always alert for leads to contact. It depends on your product or service but let's look at some prospecting sources:

Telephone directory	Yellow Pages
Thompsons	Newspapers
Backs of lorries	Planning departments
Situations vacant	Professional bodies
Schools	Colleges
Adverts seen	Hoardings
Existing client base	Exhibitions/trade fairs
Dunn and Bradstreet	Old record cards
Other salesmen	Trade journals
Leaflets received	Referrals
Local library	Chamber of Commerce
Friends and family	Clubs
Canvass blitz	Eyes and ears.

Each of these has its strengths and weaknesses. Yellow Pages has the great strength of listing businesses in groups, which is useful in mailshot preparation. However, they give no reliable indication of the size of the company, nor can you find contact names. Another risk is that businesses may have closed between copy date and publication date. Situations Vacant columns may reveal expansion plans which could herald the need for new equipment, furniture or services. Planning applications can indicate similar needs. Reference libraries usually contain all manner of directories, Yellow Pages, Kelly's, Yearbooks, trade journals, newspapers, even planning applications. It is wise to browse just to establish what is available.

Other salesmen can be a useful source of leads. If you know a salesman who sells into the same environment as you, an exchange of information can be mutually beneficial. Sellers of telephone systems, vending machines, stationery, computers, office furniture, franking machines and office cleaning services could all benefit from exchanges of leads. Useful advice such as whom to see, whom to avoid, best days to call and other data can save hours of groundwork.

Once you have decided on your list, your next step is to plan your telesales campaign. Assuming your objective is to sell the appointment, there are three basic rules:

> Give the recipient some reason to want to see you.
> Have a polished objection handling procedure.
> Fix a definite time.

Seems simple enough. To achieve no. 1, there must be a well considered Initial Benefit Statement (IBS). Many financial services canvass calls begin with the benefit of 'saving you money'. This is good in its intention but the delivery often sounds glib. When the recipient replies with the standard objection, 'I'm not interested', the reply can be, 'You're not interested in saving money?' Again, good in its intention but it frequently comes across as rather too clever, even patronising.

The prospect can feel slightly cornered. The reaction can then be hostile. An old adage in sales is, 'Win argument, lose sale'. Agreeability or harmony is always the salesman's goal. Confrontation kills. In the above example and in others we'll look at, the old tried and tested formula of *feel – felt – found* works wonders:

'I'm not interested.'

'I understand how you *feel*, Mr Prospect, and a number of our clients have *felt* exactly the same. However they have *found* that by allowing us just a brief appointment to demonstrate some of the many money- saving benefits of — they were very happy with the information we could provide. Now when would be the best time to come and see you? Mornings or evenings?'

My Cable TV friend uses this very successfully.

'Cable Television? I'm not really interested.'

'Yes, Mr Smith, I understand how you *feel* and a number of your neighbours *felt* exactly the same. However they *found* when they could see the vast range of entertainment and educational benefits our company provides, they were delighted with the service. Now could you spare me a few minutes on Monday or would later in the week suit you better?'

An alternative is to use yourself, as in:

'Double glazing? Not interested.'

'I know how you *feel*, Mr Smith. I *felt* exactly the same myself but after I had it installed my family and I *found* we were thrilled that our warm home actually cost less. But you'll need some details. When is the best time for you?'

The beauty of *feel – felt – found* is that it has a very agreeable flow to it. Once you remember the feel the other two follow quite naturally.

An Initial Benefit Statement must have some impact and credibility. While running a gym, I remember a telesales call which opened with, 'We've been able to help a number of health clubs in the area.' It sounds okay, but there were only two clubs in the city.

Or if you begin, 'We've been able to benefit several similar companies,' be prepared for, 'Oh, which ones were they?' It is not a trick question. The prospect may be genuinely interested to know.

The permutations of IBS are as varied as the number of products and services sold. The old-fashioned request for an appointment to discuss some vague 'business matter' will not work. The prospect must feel there might be some benefit or W.I.F.M. factor in the appointment. If you are only selling the appointment, the stronger and briefer the IBS the better. The more selling of the product you do on the phone the less need there is for the prospect to see you.

Planning should not only include the preparation of a good IBS, it should include preparing your desk. Do not work from directories. Transfer your list to well-prepared sheets of paper or index cards. Clear your desk of unnecessary distractions. Also consider time; Monday morning is not normally a suitable time to commence telesales.

Good record keeping is essential, even down to small details. If Susan says, 'Mr Brown is at the dentist. He won't be back till three,' write it down because after half a dozen calls you'll have completely forgotten what she said. How much more human when you call later to say, 'Ah Mr Brown, I spoke to Susan earlier and she told me you were at the dentist. Nothing serious I hope?' (Or if you want to risk a touch of humour: 'Can you speak?')

There are many examples of closing the human exchange: 'I called last week, Mr Smith, but you were in Spain. Which part were you in?'

Careful record keeping can enhance not only our professionalism but the rapport you develop as a sympathetic human being. The detail you write down on a record card at the time may seem trivial. But when trawling through your cards later on, all sorts of little prompts can give you immediate recall. *Daughter's wedding; sister's funeral; at Munich Trade Fair; golf handicap 12; in hospital; new position in company* – the list is endless.

Preparing your desk is one thing, preparing yourself is another. If you are miserable with a cold or if you've just had a row with someone, postpone it. The three greatest qualities in selling are ENTHUSIASM, CONFIDENCE and PERSISTENCE. Some salespeople prefer to make calls standing up or smiling. It does affect the vocal chords. If you don't believe it, have you ever answered the phone when in bed and the caller asked you, 'Are you in your bed?' How do they know?

Enthusiasm is attractive and contagious. Confidence works in many ways. Some salesmen rely on a firm, 'Peter Brown, please,' when the phone is answered. 'Who shall I say is calling?' 'John Smith.' The very confidence of the exchange can get you put through.

Persistence needs discipline. I once attended a lecture by Nick Sarif, a Million Dollar Round Table insurance salesman. The audience was quite cold at first. Nick went on to describe a typical day in the insurance sales office. He described how people arrive in the morning, have a coffee, chat to colleagues, make a couple of calls, look at the newspaper, make another couple of calls, another coffee and so on. The audience warmed. Nick admitted that was exactly how he ran his sales life. He went on, 'Then I bought myself a little piece of equipment which trans-formed my life and earned me a regular five-figure income. I have it here in my pocket.'

We all leaned forward, fascinated. From his pocket he produced a small hour-glass egg-timer. He explained how he disciplined himself. Every time he finished a call he turned the egg-timer over. Before the sand ran out he had to make another call. Not only did it discipline him, it also disciplined his colleagues. If they wanted to chat to him, he pointed at the hour-glass. They then made their point briefly and left him to it. No discourtesy given or taken. Nick went on consistently to make more appointments, close more sales and earn more money than any sales-person in his region.

Just as in the Fire Triangle (fig 4 overleaf) if you remove any of the three elements – Heat, Oxygen or Fuel – the fire goes out, if you remove Enthusiasm, Confidence or Perseverance, the Sales Fire also dies. A powerful quotation on persistence comes from Ray Kroc, founder of McDonald's:

> Nothing in the world can take the place of Persistence. Talent will not; nothing is more common than unsuc-cessful men with talent. Genius will not; unrewarded genius is almost a proverb. Education will not; the world is full of educated derelicts. Persistence and determination alone are omnipotent.

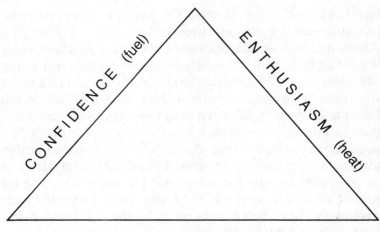

PERSISTENCE (oxygen)

Fig. 4   The Fire Triangle
(Remove any side and the fire goes out)

A convincing argument from a man who has spread McDonald's as far as Moscow.

You have combed the various directories. Your desk is prepared. *You* are prepared. (You may even have run up and down a flight of stairs or done some press-ups to pump more oxygenated blood through the brain.) You have a bright, appealing IBS ready. You are not going to have a coffee or a chat until you have completed twenty calls in a row. Just before you start, what about objections?

Generally there are only a few standard ones:

Not interested
No money
Too busy
Send me a brochure.

The knee-jerk reaction to an objection is to defend or con-front. Our objective is always harmony, so 'not interested' could be handled with, 'Yes, Mr Smith, I can appreciate you not being interested in something you haven't had a chance to evaluate fully, but so that you can judge for yourself could I call in on Monday, or perhaps later in the week might suit you better.'

No guarantee of an appointment, of course, but it will take you nearer than the knee-jerk, 'Just give me five minutes of your time.'

No money? Again agree. 'Of course Mr Smith, with the economic climate the way it is, naturally you are concerned about savings, however if I could show you how — might save you money, you'd want to know about it. But you can't judge till we've had a chat. When would . . .?'

Too busy? This actually is not a great objection, as the intimation is not 'I don't want to see you' but 'I don't have time'.

Some salesmen respond with, 'I'm very pleased to hear you are busy. Business good, then?' The implication is clear but the prospect may feel cornered and as we saw earlier, people when cornered may react hostilely.

Far better, 'We appreciate businessmen's time is very valuable, that is why we always telephone to ensure we can arrange a convenient time. Would perhaps before 9 a.m. or after 5 p.m. be more suitable for you?'

The objection was not *whether* but *when*. The prospect may then revert to *whether*, as in: 'I'm not really interested', which gives you another chance.

Send me a brochure. A frequent response to this is, 'I'll bring one in with me' or 'I'd rather talk to you personally.' Remember, what *you* would rather do is of no interest to the prospect. Try: 'It would be wrong of me, Mr Smith, to burden you with reams of literature, most of which might not be relevant to your needs. To save you time, if we have a brief appointment, I can soon pinpoint your needs and then leave you the precise literature you need. Now when . . .?' (Not that you would just be leaving a brochure, but your objective is sell that appointment.)

This leaves you to fix a definite time.

Pretty obvious, really. But perhaps not. When we obtain an appointment, we are usually very pleased. The tendency can be to say, 'Thank you Mr Smith' or 'I'll look forward to seeing you on Wednesday'. It is wiser to treat the appointment with the respect you wish the prospect to treat it:

'Right Mr Smith, I'll just put that in my diary. That's two o'clock on Thursday at your office in Queen Street. You're just off the high street, aren't you? I know the area. Fine. So I'll look forward . . .'

The 'I'll just put that in my diary' is a polite way of saying 'Please put that in *your* diary' – which could be construed as a little bit impertinent. The point of the clear confirmation of address and time is to impress on the prospect's mind that you are making a professional and fixed appointment. The more casually we treat the appointment the less importance the prospect attaches to it.

Should you phone in advance to confirm that you are coming? Generally no, as it may give the prospect a chance to cancel. If you have doubts or perhaps long distance is involved, you could always send a confirmatory note in the post. Then, if your doubts have substance, the onus is on the prospect to contact you.

The numbers game

Prospecting is sometimes call the Numbers Game or the Funnel Principle – the more volume you put in the top the more trickles out of the bottom.

Forgive a moment's digression here, but fate seems to have ordained I include this. I have just received a telephone call. It was a telesales lady from a home improvements company. She asked: 'Are you interested in changing your windows at all?'

No IBS of any sort. Just a cold closed question meriting, as it did, 'No.' I volunteered that I was moving house shortly.

'Oh – you won't be needing it then. Okay, thank you, 'bye.'

With that question, just how many calls will she have to make to gain an appointment? Even the objection could have been met with some comment on how the value of the house could be enhanced.

One could not ask for a greater illustration of the *quantity* versus *quality* argument. As the quality increases so the quantity can reduce. Experienced insurance (and other) salespeople can acquire a broad client bank which, along with referrals, can keep them busy. However, even with excellent quality there will always be a need for a 'Funnel' topping-up exercise every so often.

The key to financial success in sales is to know your Ratios. If in order to earn £500 per week you have to contact an average of 250 people, then each prospect is worth £2. The benefit of this logic is that you plan effective goal-setting. It gives you structure. Every sales office has written on a wall somewhere:

You don't plan to fail. You fail to plan.

When you set out your Year Planner don't make the obvious mistake of planning over 52 weeks. Knock off three or four for holidays, another one for Bank Holidays, perhaps another one or two for special events or sickness. Then fix your daily call rate. The beauty of knowing your ratios is that it reduces our greatest fear: rejection. Every time you are told, 'No thank you' (or worse), you can compensate with, 'Fine, that's another £2 to me'. Even if it takes a ratio of 500 calls to earn £500, at least you know the volume of work required. Initially the number may be great but with time the ratio always improves. It is also important to subdivide your ratios: How many telephone calls to each appointment? How many appointments to each closing opportunity? How may closes to each order?

Knowing your subdivided ratios helps you analyse your selling strengths and weaknesses. If perhaps your ratio of telephone calls to appointments was above par but your appointments to closing opportunities was below par, then some analysis of your interview technique is necessary. Some salespeople are brilliant on the telephone, others only excel when face-to-face. Don't abandon your weak points, concentrating on your strong; analyse what the good tele-salespeople are doing and practise or train until you are as good or better. If not, a mental block can develop, which with the passing of time can be difficult to shift.

Goal setting

Once you know your ratios, accurate goal setting is made easier. If you plan to attend the World Cup, take the family on the holiday of a lifetime or buy something substantial like a house, car or boat, first evaluate the cost, then work backwards. If you need, say, an extra £5,000 in a year, you may need to sell ten extra boxes in the year or one extra per month. You know that for every two closes you make you get one order. You also know you might need eight inter-view situations to reach two closing opportunities. You could need forty canvass calls to make eight appointments. That is ten a week or two extra a day. Can this be done? No great difficulty here, so the goal is realistic.

Many new (and not so new) salespeople when asked their sales objectives say, 'I'm going to make lots of money.'

'How are you going to achieve that?'

'I'm going to work all the hours God gives me.'

An admirable sentiment and an excellent attitude, but without a clear structure based on known ratios and realis-tic goal setting, disillusion and disappointment can set in. Each rejection can build up a cumulative effect of loss of heart. Whereas with known ratios, even if your daily target of calls all meet rejection you know your score rate must average out. The bonus to look forward to is that with time and experience the ratios always improve.

Time management

Working harder is not always the key to success. Working smarter often is. We all know the obvious pitfalls of having one appointment in the north of a patch then the next in the south. Good time and territory management is all about grouping similar tasks and geographic visits together.

We have all experienced the panic of dashing from A to B, then remembering you have to get a proposal written and get to the dry cleaners and so on. Too many miles to cover and not enough hours in the day.

The most effective method of time management is a brainstorm. Sit down, perhaps on a Sunday, and just pour over every conceivable task for the week ahead onto a sheet of paper. Scatter them all over the sheet and ring them.

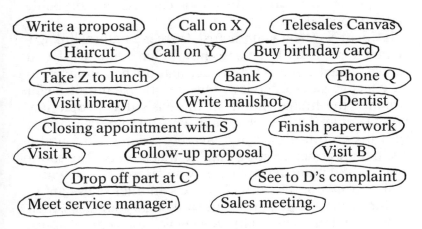

The list can be quite extensive. The beauty of committing your tasks to paper is that you clear your mind. Nothing is worse than going round clicking your fingers muttering, 'I *must* call X' or 'Remind me to ring Mr Y.' Unless you relieve the pressure of your memory bank you can create stress and even physically give yourself a headache. We've all seen the disorganised salesman or – more often –

manager who cannot walk in a straight line without smacking hand to forehead and exclaiming, 'Oh dammit, I forget to . . .', often blaming someone else: 'Susan, why didn't you remind me?'

If you know you have committed every possible task to paper, the pressure in your mind reduces. Your next task is:

Prioritise and link

Some people take seven sheets of paper headed with the days of the week. They then lift off task after task and allocate them to a specific day. Linking is where you look at the tasks scattered all over the sheet of paper and make logical linkage. The day you 'Finish paperwork' would be a sensible day to do your 'Telephone canvass' and probably 'Write proposal.'

If Client X is near your dentist, there is a natural linkage. Which to see first? It depends how much dental work you expect to have done. A frozen face may not be conducive to an effective sales interview. On the other hand, it might enhance the human bond on the basis that People buy From People. (I knew a salesman who did some canvassing with his arm in plaster and wearing a sling. He found a distinctly warmer greeting than he was used to. The spontaneous and immediate reaction was, 'Here's a man with a broken arm' not the normal, 'Here's another salesman'.)

Once you have prioritised and linked all your tasks, then enter the lot into your diary. Also make 'forerunner' notes. These remind you of any preparation you may need to make: 'Meeting with client X first thing tomorrow. Remember to take home . . .'

It is surprising the number of people – particularly managers – who dash out of an office shouting, 'I've got a meeting with the MD in five minutes. Has anyone seen my . . .?' Yet the meeting has been in his diary for several days. A 'forerunner' note could have saved all that panic (not to mention the disruption of everybody else's work).

One final guideline on time management. Do allow time. Phoning ahead to other appointments saying you are running late is often unavoidable; however, it is equally often avoidable. Leave blanks or what is now known by the Filofax types as 'White space' or 'Windows'. (I still have to smile when I hear people say, 'I have a window on Wednesday' – but, what's in a name?)

5

THE SALES INTERVIEW

'I am very busy but I could spare you ten minutes on Wednesday.'

You have an appointment. Good. You feel good about yourself and your company. Your product knowledge is comprehensive. You know all the features of your product or service and you can translate them into benefits because you have done some research into the company on which you are calling. You know the position in the company of the person you are meeting. Now you can plan. What to bring? Samples; a 'V' display board; testimonials from satisfied customers; a sight seller; someone else, perhaps a service manager; finished work of your product – only you can decide.

What is the objective? To close the sale? To fix a further meeting to make a presentation? An invitation to a demonstration? To be placed on an Approved Suppliers list? The opportunity to tender or submit a proposal? To exchange pleasantries and have a cup of coffee?

The stages of a sales presentation are represented by many formulae and acronyms. We'll just look at two because all are variations of the same theme.

(a) Establish the need.
    Prove you can meet the need.
    Justify your price.

How is this best achieved, thoroughly and professionally? As good a way as any is embodied in the simple
acronym.

(b) I.D.E.A.
   (Information – Dislikes and Likes – Effect – Agreement)

Let's work backwards. Ideally you wish to obtain *agreement* that some change in the existing service or product
is necessary. You will only obtain an agreement once you
have discovered the adverse *effects* of the existing system.
Before you explore the adverse effects of the present
equipment you need to probe every area for *dislikes and
likes*. First and foremost we need a solid bank of
information.

Failure to achieve a broad enough base of information
loses more sales than an inability to close. The key to establishing a comprehensive base of information is good probing skills.

Not long ago I thought I'd take up tennis. I went into a
sports shop. As customers we seldom say, 'I want to buy
a . . .'; we tend to say something non-committal like, 'I
thought I might just have a look at some tennis racquets'.
The sales (I use the word loosely) assistant showed me a
'good' one and named a price. Then she showed me a
'better' one, naming a higher price. Finally she showed me
'quite an expensive' one, conceding it was a 'bit dear'. You
guessed it, I didn't buy. The irony was, I had the cash and
was quite prepared to buy. I may even have joined the long
list of 'time-wasters' she meets.

The unasked Probing Questions (which are not a skill,
just plain common sense) are obvious to any salesperson:
How good is your game? How long have you been playing?
How regularly do you plan to play? How big is your grip?
What do you know about tennis racquets? Try this grip for
size (involve the prospect with hands-on where possible).
If I knew the product better I could probably list several
more questions. Had she *(i) established the need*, she

could very comfortably have gone on to the next stage, *(ii)* *prove you can meet the need*, by telling me she knew exactly the type of racquet which was most suitable. Throw in some product knowledge and perhaps a testimonial – 'This is an excellent racquet, made of whatever, weighs so many ounces, light with a powerful delivery. My brother/friend/whoever uses one and swears by it' – and all that would remain would be *(iii) justify your price*. It is an excellent bargain/very good value for money at £ . . .

The interesting thing about probing skills is that if you ask any group of salespeople what questions they would ask in certain selling situations (other than their own product), they usually come up with a very logical and perceptive list.

For example, a vending machine salesman would want to know . . . what? The following list is the product of a one-minute brainstorm. (Close your eyes for a moment if you wish and see what questions you might come up with.) How many staff are there? What seems to be the greatest preference, tea, coffee, orange, etc? Have you set breaks or is it just a 'help yourself' policy? What system do you use at present? Boiling a kettle – who does that? How often? Where is the sink?

Working through I.D.E.A., we've got most of the basic information. Let's move on to D – Dislikes and Likes. How many mugs do you use? Who washes them? Who buys the tea, coffee, etc? Who buys the washing-up liquid? Who collects the money? How many breakages/spillages do you have?

Just a word on likes. Be prepared for them. In the above scenario, people might express a liking for freshly brewed tea-bags. If you cannot match the like, find as many dislikes with the present system to outweigh the like.

Having acquired the basic information along with the dislikes and likes, the less professional salesman would try and close with the features and benefits of his product. However, the fully professional will probe for the Effects:

'How much time is wasted waiting for the kettle to boil?'

'What could staff be doing instead of washing cups?'

'How big a nuisance is shopping for ingredients?'

'How messy do you find all these cups, milk bottles, sugar bags, etc?'

'How big a nuisance is drawing petty cash or having a whip-round for money?'

'How big a problem is sugar granules on the floor?'

These are all Effect questions. Dislike and Like questions are very valuable and could be sufficient to move on with to the close. However, they are often factual and may not extract the more powerful emotional reasons as to why people buy. Effect questions, however, involve the emotions. Irritants, nuisances, wastes of time and money – these are stronger motivational forces for buying.

A direct comparison can be drawn with the sale of motor cars. Information questions might include:

'What are you driving at the moment?'

'How long have you had that?'

'Did you buy it new or second hand – cash or lease?'

'Is it the estate or saloon – engine size?'

and so on. You'll need personal details to Establish the Need:

'What do you use the car for . . . business?'

'Family size? Who'll be driving? Recreation involved?'

etc.

Dislikes and likes:

'Why did you buy that at the time?'

'What problems have you had with it?' (None? – find some.)

'How do you find the rear wheel drive in bad weather?'

Probing can continue for low acceleration, instability in wind, poor handling, fuel economy, noise, service intervals, breakdowns and a host of other factors from a poor radio to a vulnerable aerial.

You could leave it at that and head straight for the

Features and Benefits of the model you had in mind. Far better to probe for effects.

It is not so much a breakdown which involves the emotions. It is the effect – a three-mile walk in the rain; being late for an important appointment; sitting in a lay-by for an hour. Low acceleration is factual. The heart skipping a beat while overtaking a long vehicle or even cutting a dash at the traffic lights – these evoke the emotions. Some books on sales actually quantify the emotional and rational in buying as 84 per cent emotion and 16 per cent rational. How on earth anyone can quantify these so precisely I fail to see, but the point is well made.

Insurance people go through a 'fact find'. They gain Information in order to establish the need by ascertaining family size, ages, present cover, income and commitments. Dislikes could lie with an existing policy or lack of it. The Effect card can be played quite strongly by probing the consequences of inadequate cover in the event of job loss, sickness, damage or death. A question like, 'Tell me John – sorry to have to raise it, but what provision have you made for Mary and the children in the event of . . .?' will have much more effect than the more factual 'What cover have you at present?'

Once the I.D.E of I.D.E.A has been covered the A. for Agreement is much more easily obtained. However, it is essential to recap.

The prelude to closing for an agreement is a summary.

'So, let's just recap Mr Smith. Your existing equipment is eight years old. You are experiencing problems with A, B and C. It is constantly jamming necessitating quite lengthy repairs. Because of its age, some spare parts are no longer available which often causes delays. Its function is too complicated which means you need a dedicated operator or considerable training for a replacement operator. You are concerned that the Safety Officer may not pass it at the next inspection. The effects of these problems are that you are losing valuable time and have been behind with the orders on several occasions. This in turn has cost you money and some damage to your reputation.'

Depending on the scenario, this summary can be longer or shorter but the objective is to seek agreement. The time honoured phrase in sales has always been: 'So if we can show you a way to—you'd be interested, yes?' If the I.D.E. have been covered thoroughly and professionaly, the A. for Agreement should be almost automatic.

The amateur will find one or two areas of Dissatisfaction and go for a close as quickly as possible. 'So you'll be wanting a new machine, then?'

This can and does work, but not as often as thorough professional probing. It is often the quality of the salesman's questions more than his answers that influence the buyer. *Telling is not selling.* We looked earlier at the failure of the old-fashioned spiel which was all telling.

My partner and I once sat in front of the MD of a manufacturing company for two and a half hours. Our objective was to sell him Sales Training. We asked question after question. We had read all his company's literature beforehand so our questions reflected a certain understanding of his business. We asked about his salesforce – numbers, ages, experience, background, training or lack of it. Two questions in particular had the most powerful effect. One was, 'What percentage of your sales is order-taking and what percentage would you call actual selling?', followed by, 'What percentage of the market share have you got?'

After the second question the MD sat back in his chair, reflected for a moment or two and then said, 'I see what you mean.'

We had actually *told* him nothing, but the calibre of the questions was such that he could deduce the answers for himself. He conceded that as much as 80 per cent of his sales was order-taking and he had 37 per cent of quite a specialist market. The deduction was simple: if he could double his sales effort to 40 per cent actual selling, how much larger would his slice of the market share be.

The MD asked us hardly any questions at all about ourselves, our experience, our company, our training. He did ask our fees, which we justified; then he concluded with 'When can you start?'

Gaining information

So the first objective is to gain information. To introduce this subject to salesmen I often ask them who in their opinion is the best interviewer on television. Answers normally include well-known celebrities such as Wogan, Aspel, or Day.

Often their interpretation of the question is who is the *best known* interviewer on TV, so their answers in that context could be correct. When the question is defined as, 'What is the objective of the interviewer and who is the best?' the answers vary. On the premise that the objective of the interviewer is to obtain information, a celebrity is not necessary and the focus must be on the interviewee.

The job of the celebrity interviewer is not too difficult as most of the guests are also celebrities and are only too keen to plug their latest movie, record or book. The job of the serious interviewer is quite different. His job is to extract precise information from people who more often than not are reluctant to give it. Watch investigative journalists pursue suspected embezzlers, dishonest businessmen or politicians on issues they would rather evade. The skill (or lack of it) of the interviewer becomes apparent. Getting Peter Ustinov to recount some early experiences would be child's play compared with asking Ernest Saunders or the late Robert Maxwell to account for some of the more interesting aspects of their business affairs.

The salesman's role model is the serious interviewer. One of the all time greats as an interviewer is Alan Whicker. There is nothing ostentatious about the man.

Sober suit, mild non-judgemental manner, very good questions and effective body language. He asks a good question. The interviewee answers. Whicker rests his hand on his face, partially covering his mouth and just nods. The interviewee continues speaking, then stops. Whicker tilts his head to one side and says 'Uh-huh' and the speaker carries on. Frequently the producer edits the interviewer out of the film, just leaving the talking head of the interviewee. Professional interviewing at its best.

Even when the interviewee says something quite outrageous – you may recall the ex-pat Pom in Australia who made offensive racial comments – Whicker just nodded. Had he conveyed any element of censure the interviewee would have clammed up. No doubt Whicker is as fair minded a man as any but it was not his job to fault or condemn. His job was to extract information.

A senior policeman told me that one of the difficult tasks in questioning a suspect is not to convey the disgust and hostility policemen often feel in some of their uglier cases. Being judgemental inhibits the interviewee to the point where information ceases. When information ceases, the task of the interviewer has failed. One way round this in certain circumstances is to alternate interviewers: the police regularly use the 'Mr Nasty and Mr Nice Guy' routine.

Alan Whicker is as good a role model as a salesman can find. Not only is he always smart, courteous, calm, non-confrontational, but he invariably asks perceptive open questions.

Before we carry on let us look at some types of questions: closed questions, open questions, reflective questions, loaded questions, rhetorical questions.

In effect the salesperson only uses the first three. The road to an early grave is paved with *closed questions*. Yet sometimes, when we are under pressure, for example when the buyer says something like, 'Listen, I'm very busy. I can only give you a few minutes', we respond with, 'Right, I just need a few details. Do you have a widget at present?'

'Yes.'
'Have you had it long?' – 'No.'
'Do you lease it?' – 'No.'
'Did you buy it, then?' – 'Yes.'
'Do you find it okay?' – 'Yes.'

We know this type of exchange could go on for ever. In reality of course, the buyer is seldom this unhelpful but it still makes the interview very hard work when one question – 'Can you tell me something about your existing widget?' – could probably obtain all the information in one go. Even if the buyer were to reply, 'Well, we've had it for five years,' then stop, a calm 'Uh-huh' with appropriate 'I'm not speaking' body language will encourage him to carry on.

The beauty of *open questions* is that not only can you obtain much more information per question but it also takes the pressure off the salesperson. While the buyer is giving a fuller answer you have the luxury of being able to consider an intelligent next question, whereas with meagre Yes and No replies the formulation time for the next question is minimal and the quality of the question suffers.

Closed questions can be very helpful in a sales interview when wishing to change tack or in seeking agreement, as in, 'Have you had any difficulties with your existing supplier?' If 'Yes', then off we go again probing – 'Tell me about that' or 'What type of difficulties?' 'What about service/call out times?' or some other specific.

'Well, we did have a problem with . . .'

'Oh, tell me about that – when, how often', etc. Seek the information, then establish the effect.

Multiple questions can be a risk. If you ask several questions in a row, the prospect may answer only one or be confused as to your direction. There is a type of multiple question that can be helpful in getting the prospect talking (or 'on a runner' as it is sometimes known). For example, you ask a prospect to tell you about his existing system and he counters with, 'What do you want to know?' Here a multiple question can be more effective than a single one: 'Well, in order to establish how my company can be of assistance to you, I need to know about your existing system such as its use, how old it is, who supplied it, how it copes with your existing work load, how the key operators find it – that sort of thing.'

Normally a buyer will help with, 'Let's see, now. When we installed it three years ago, we needed to . . .'

If he does start 'on a runner', it makes the salesman's job so much easier. He can listen (and *show* he is listening), think, formulate his next question, make mental or written notes and act in the role of professional consultant rather than just the glib salesman delivering a spiel.

Any other professional, whether lawyer, doctor or clergyman, expects to listen in some detail before he or she can begin to offer professional advice. The most effective way of adopting this role is to put down your *goalposts* clearly at the beginning. Far too many salespeople launch straight into a sales interview with a series of questions. By the time the salesman reaches question four or five the prospect may become defensive or even hostile.

Goalposts are important in presentations, meetings and job interviews. The bad manager will conduct a job interview without goalposts. The job applicant is bombarded with a series of questions, often becoming more tense or nervous because he or she has no control and consequently cannot see which direction the interview is taking. The good manager would place the goalposts first.

'Right Susan, take a seat. What I'd like to do is run through your CV, asking you a few questions, just to see what you have done with your career to date. Then I'll tell you about the job and the company you would be working for. After that you ask me any questions you like and we'll have a general chat. How does that appear to you?'

The individual is consulted and not diminished and the interview now has structure.

The salesman should begin with a good IBS (Initial Benefit Statement). Then place the goalposts:

'Mr Smith, we have been able to help a number of companies such as yours with their (problem). Precisely how much benefit we can be to your company I can't say until I have a bit more information. So I need to ask you a few questions about your existing system, its use, efficiency, problems etc., and I'll take a few notes as we go along. Can I just ask you a few general questions about the company . . .?'

Beginning with a few general questions about the company is doubly useful. Firstly from a business standpoint it is important to know precisely who you are talking to. Is he or she the DMU (Decsion Making Unit) or only part of it? How long has the company been in business will be necessary if your product involves leasing. Credit clearance has become more difficult and for new businessess almost impossible without a personal guarantee. Other factors can be essential such as central or local buying policy, budget, other branches and so on. In the general introduction you may be lucky enough to catch a *buying signal*. 'Yes we've just moved into these premises and we need a new system as soon as possible.' Music!

The second benefit of a general introductory chat is that it allows an opportunity for the cementing of the human bond. We saw in Chapter 2 that we sell four things: yourself – your product/service – your company – your price. If each one had a weight then logically the product/service would be the heaviest because that is what the prospect actually buys. However, chronologically, *yourself* is the most important because if you don't sell *you*, you may not get the opportunity to sell the other three.

In domestic sales the same principle applies with perhaps even greater strength. Inviting someone into your office is distinct from inviting someone into your home. Kitchen sales, replacement windows or insurance should all involve a general chat to start the conversational ball rolling: How long in the house? How do they like the area? New job? Promotion? How did the children take the move? Where from? How long there? All these questions and many more are fertile soil for human exchange. Once the *you* bond has been formed, any transaction becomes easier. In Chapter 3 the question was posed: how often have you walked out of a shop because you did not like the sales assistant and his or her manner? (An American friend of mine has a name for British sales assistants. He calls them Sales Prevention Officers. It was he who suggested that replacing some stores' staff with honesty boxes would actually increase their takings.)

Whether direct sales, retail sales, a job interview, a presentation or a bank loan the *you* sale is vital. The old adage, You Don't Get a Second Chance to Make a First Impression, is advice which is now more important than ever. As products and services become more and more standard, the calibre of the sales people becomes crucial. Pubs and restaurants with individuality and a friendly landlord or restaurateur who remembers your name do thriving business. Price is almost an irrelevance.

Note taking

In many sales situations the taking of notes is not necessary but in others it is essential. What is the objective of the interview? Let us assume the objective is to obtain an agreement that some improvement is necessary with an existing system. The close we are after is the time-honoured, 'So if I can show you a way to ... you'd be interested, yes?'

The prelude to a close for agreement is the summary. If you have a flawless memory with instant and accurate recall you may not need to take notes to deliver a comprehensive summary. (Though you should still take notes as there are other benefits which we shall look at in a moment.) Clear concise notes make the summary impressive.

In the health club sale we used a fact-find analysis sheet. We began with an IBS then laid the goalposts.

'We've been getting some great results for our members but before we can suggest a programme for you, we need to know about your requirements. We cater for people who wish to lose weight, gain muscle definition or keep fit. What was it you were interested in doing? Lose weight and keep fit, right. What weight are you?' Then we were off. Question after question, with a few reflective questions thrown in: 'Really? As much as that?'

All leading to the summary:

'Right, let's see now. You need to lose forty-eight pounds of excess fatty tissue. This is stored mainly in the waist, abdomen, hip and thigh. Your muscle tone is poor, particularly in the pectorals in the chest. Your breathing . . . Your posture . . . You feel sluggish after a day in the . . .'

You get the picture. An agreement would be obtained at each stage of the summary. (This is sometimes know as The Ladder of Yeses.) Having obtained a series of Yeses on each requirement then the final closing Yes is easier to obtain.

This was the first of the classic Three Stages of a Sale which are worth repeating: Establish the need – Prove you can meet the need – Justify the price.

Having gained agreement that the prospect wished to achieve the results, Stage Two was to explain how a programme was planned: 'First of all we take your weight and measurements. Then we give you a fitness test to check the Three Ss – your Strength, Stamina and Suppleness. We check your pulse rate before and after exercise. Then we can plan a programme tailor-made for you.' Explanation of the programme followed, stressing the ease, the results and benefits to the prospect.

Stage Three, the price, was always sold on the basis of what the Americans were the first to call 'Reducing to the

Ridiculous'. 'So all these results and the benefits of a lean healthy body can be obtained for less than you spend on cigarettes.' Or less per week than the prospect spends on a round of drinks. Or the amount of junk food the prospect cuts down on would pay for the membership.

The financial service sale uses exactly the same principle using a similar fact-find sheet:

'Right Mr Smith, we have helped provide many similar families with the security they need along with tax-efficient savings plans, but I'll need a few brief details . . .' Then appropriate information questions – salary, mortgage, size of family, ages: establish the need. Then the summary: "You're aged . . . your health is A1. You are a non-smoker. You want to ensure Susan and the children are covered in the event of death/illness/unemployment . . .' Next, prove you can meet the need with the Features, Advantages and Benefits (FAB) of your product. Finally sell your price.

The first benefit of taking notes is that it allows you to make a clear concise summary. The second benefit is that it can help provide an effective cost comparison. Fax salesmen in the early days used this with powerful effect:

'Let's see now, Mr Smith. Your quarterly telephone bill is £X. You reckon up to half of this is wasted through delays in being connected to the correct person or in non-business chat. A substantial saving could also be made in using off-peak call time. Your staff spend a considerable amount of time receiving or placing orders on the telephone. You spend about £Y on courier services for urgent documents. You spend £Z on postage not including cost of stationery, envelopes and staff time . . .' With such a thorough and professional cost comparison, the agreement close was easy: 'So, if I could show you a way to . . . and actually save you money you'd be interested, yes?'

A third benefit of note taking is that it lends an element of seriousness and professionalism to the interview. But first you must be professional. A young man in white socks, Ian Botham haircut and flecky suit cannot expect to close the

You door effectively, whether he takes notes or not. Taking notes shows you are interested in what the buyer tells you. It also impresses the buyer that you listen to and record accurately what he tells you. Do take clear and constructive notes. The pads of many salesmen often have words scattered at random mixed in with the odd squiggle or doodle. One useful method is to draw bold asterisks against those points which you feel will be valuable in your summary.

A fourth benefit of note taking is that it can reduce pressure. In a one-to-one situation across a desk, it can feel somewhat confrontational. You wish to appear relaxed. You want to deliver a reasonable IBS, place your goalposts, ask information questions, keep good eye contact, listen (and appear to listen), formulate your next question, steer towards (or away from) a certain topic and remember facts and figures. If you are already under some pressure you can almost feel a sense of panic. (Show me the salesman who has not experienced this.) The note pad or clip-board can alleviate all this. By breaking eye contact every so often and recording some information you allow a few precious moments to collect your thoughts.

Professional selling always recognises that telling is not selling. There is of course a place for telling but that is Stage Two where we prove we can meet the need.

Selling has been described as 'One mind influencing another'. In order for one mind to influence another the foundation for good human relations must be laid. The old fashioned, 'Have I got a deal for you!' or 'Good Morning sir, I represent ABC Ltd and I'd like to tell you about the wonderful range of . . .' can and do still work, but the percentage rate of success is minimal compared with the professional, structured approach. Again, it is not really a skill but a mixture of pure logic and good People Skills.

Incidentally, there is one organisation which relies on cold-calling, yet despite vast experience it seems never to have learnt that telling is not selling – the Jehovah's

Witnesses. Generally their reluctance to listen or ask questions and their level of product knowledge is as such to render their message ineffective.

Good questioning is essential. Not only the type of question but the quality. Some salesmen when following up a lead will open with, 'What sort of computer/filing cabinet/copier/widget were you thinking of?'

It's not bad. It does get straight to the point but it is just too direct. The prospect may not really have a clue. He may also be reluctant to display too much ignorance. He may counter with a wry, 'A cheap one'. A bad start. It is much safer to adhere to the basics: IBS; goalposts; questions.

Even if the prospect quotes a model number, it is still wiser – and more professional – to check. 'Fine Mr Smith, my company is very keen on good service and part of my job is to make quite sure the model matches exactly the customer's requirements. Can I just check . . .' Straight into a Probing exercise. Should the prospect be quite certain about a model, its functions and the application, no harm done and his respect for you and your professionalism will be enhanced. Doubly so if the model quoted was inappropriate to his needs.

We have looked at open questions and closed questions. Let's examine *reflective questions*.

A reflective question is where you reflect back a word or words a prospect has used or just use a comment like, 'Really?' or 'As often as that?'

Using the prospect's own words is very effective as it is non-intrusive, it avoids misinterpretation and shows you are listening. For example the prospect says:

We have had one or two problems with our present system.'

'Problems?'

'Yes, and on one occasion it took the service people two days to get here.'

'Two days?'

'Yes, it was a nightmare . . .'

Obviously you cannot use reflective questions continuously or the prospect may begin to wonder if there is a parrot in the room. We will use open questions more often than not as in 'What type of problems?' or 'Why did it take so long?' but the reflective 'Problems?' can help the prospect's flow. Ideally the balance of talk initially should be very much in the prospect's favour.

Question-hopping can distract the prospect. If he is 'on a runner', leave him. With intelligent course correction you can gain all the necessary information.

One aspect of nerves is that sometimes we can turn an open question into a closed one. A copier salesman asked a prospect an excellent open question: 'Tell me, Mr Smith, what do you use your present copier for?' The prospect sat back and thought for a moment. Because the salesman was tense, the few seconds' pause was too much for him so he added, 'Is it just the usual office bits and pieces?'

The prospect, perhaps relieved of his mental task, replied, 'Yes, I suppose so.'

Had the salesman waited a moment longer he might have obtained all the information he sought – paper sizes, invoices, mailshots and so on. An even better open question would have been a *multiple prompt*.

'Can you tell me about your existing copier. How many copies you do, what paper sizes, what features it has and what you use them for – that sort of thing?'

The danger with closed questions is that you can get caught in a stream of them and find it difficult to break out. For instance, in the above situation, where the prospect says 'Yes, I suppose so', because the ball is so quickly returned to your court you may give a knee-jerk reaction with another closed question and another:

'Do you copy mainly A4?'

'Yes.'

'What about A3?'

'No, not much.'

'Do you use it yourself?'

'No.'
and so on. Hard work.

Assistant buyer

A number of professional sales organisations encourage
their salespeople to be seen as Assistant Buyers. In a one-
to-one sales interview, the very layout of the meeting can be
seen as adversarial. Two contestants either side of a desk.
The salesman cannot physically draw his chair round to
the buyer's side so they both are physically and metaphori-
cally 'on the same side'. To reduce the severe 180 degree
angle, it is wise to draw the chair slightly to one side,
reducing the angle to 135 degrees.

Good use of language can help 'unite' the buyer and
seller:

'The best thing *we* can do here is . . .'
'The last thing *we* want is poor service . . .'
'I think here *we* are probably looking at . . .'
'What sort of delivery date are *we* looking at . . .'
'A service agreement will give *us* the back-up *we* need.'

The objective is avoid too much 'you' and 'I' but to try to
create an atmosphere where you both appear to be looking
at the same problem.

Incident recollection

In the I.D.E.A. structured sale we first seek the Information,
then areas of Dislike or Dissatisfaction, then the Effects of
those Dissatisfactions. Working on the principle that we
wish to involve the emotions, an excellent lever is to seek an
incident. For instance, in an advertising space sale, you
might have asked how happy the prospect was with his
existing medium, with such specifics as misprints or late/
missed insertions. He could tell you he has had one or two

problems. You probe the type of problem, then go for the Effect: 'What effect did that have on your business?'

'It was a bit of a nuisance.'

Not terribly emotional. You would have preferred it if he had said, 'Effect? I'll tell you what effect. It was a complete disaster.'

So you could go for an incident. You ask for a specific occasion or occasions when misprints occurred or adverts were omitted. If you can get the prospect to relive in his mind an incident when there was a strong irritation or anger factor, the Dissatisfaction element could be powerful enough for him to seek satisfaction elsewhere.

The remaining types of question – *loaded* and *rhetorical* – do not really enter into the salesman's repetoire. Loaded in salesman's language really means 'trial closing' (Chap 8).

An early question in a car showroom might be, 'When were you thinking of changing your car?'

The nervous or suspicious prospect might reply, 'Who said I was thinking of changing?' But normally he'll use slight evasion, such as. 'Not for a month or so.'

Good. At least you know he is definitely in the market.

Or an estate agent might ask, 'How soon will you need your new home?'

A vending machine salesman: 'Where were you thinking of siting the machine?'

'In that corner there,' would be a very satisfactory answer.

'Is it your policy to lease or to pay by cash purchase?'

'I'll be paying cash.' Thank you very much.

Rhetorical questions are those used for emphasis and do not need an answer:

'The last thing you'll want is an unreliable machine, right?'

'Expensive advertising which nobody reads is something you can do without, yes?'

One final benefit of intelligent, perceptive questioning is that it counteracts the dangers of stereotyping. The image

82

of the old-fashioned amateur salesman still persists in people's minds. Yesterday's fast-talking, uncaring, always *telling* salesman merits rejection. By asking questions, listening, checking and showing genuine interest, the modern professional breaks away from the stereotypical image, becomes more acceptable and – most importantly – closes more sales.

6

NEGOTIATION SKILLS

Objection handling

Objections can occur at the beginning of a sale, at any time during the sale or at the very end.

The first objections we looked at were when telephone canvassing. The sale of a product or service is of paramount importance to us. To the prospect it is nowhere near the top of his list of priorities, unless his present system has become completely useless and the purchase of a new one is urgent. In this instance he, no doubt, will already have made some enquiries and it is probably too late.

Larger corporations may have someone or a department dedicated to buying. The Buyer or Acquisitions Manager may agree to see you, simply because that is part of his or her job. Salespeople familiar with major accounts know that this can be a long process. The period from being vetted and accepted to the actual placing of an order can be anything from six to eighteen months.

With smaller businesses your product or service may be of no urgent appeal to the decision maker. He might be in the market if only you could get a chance to see him and make a convincing presentation. But because of the lack of immediate need the buyer may take the quickest option and dismiss you with: 'Send me some literature'; 'I'm too busy'; or 'I'm not interested'. Quite possibly the buyer could benefit from your product but it is neither pressing nor near the top of his priority list, so he chooses to brush you off. Hence the three criteria for successful telephone canvassing are:

Give the buyer some reason to want to see you
Have a polished Objection Handling procedure
Fix a definite time.

We looked at telephone objections and the use of Feel, Felt, Found in Chapter Four. The main ingredient was harmony and the avoidance of confrontation. So it is when cold-canvassing on foot. In kitchen sales, the homeowners might say they were not really interested. The knee-jerk reaction is to reply, 'But if you'll only allow me a few minutes . . .' or try to counter the objection in some way.

Another meaning of 'counter' is 'against'. The very word has a confrontational ring to it. The essence of good negotiation is to acknowledge the other party's point of view: 'Yes, I understand how you *feel*, in fact a number of our customers *felt* exactly the same, but when they *found* how the new kitchen enhanced the value of their home and their lives and how easy payment was, they were delighted. Allow me at least to give you a few details.' The success percentage will always be relatively small but much higher than the old-fashioned foot-in-the-door approach.

Another type of objection is where you encounter a degree of hostility on a cold call. The prospect asks what company you are from and then shows you to the door (or worse). There is a little sequence which could help here: *Pre-empt – Listen – Cushion – Focus – Agree – Overcome.*

Firstly, if calling on an existing or ex-customer, it is always wise to check through any customer service records. If you are new to the patch try to check if anything is known about him. The last thing you want is to walk in with a friendly smile to a customer and be told that he said he never wanted to see 'you people' on his premises again.

So where possible, *pre-empt* any confrontation. If there is a bad customer relations situation, you can still call but your approach would be quite different. An advance telephone call might run (assuming you can get through):

'Mr Smith, I'm Peter Brown from ABC Ltd.'

'ABC Ltd? I'm not at all happy with you people.'

'That's exactly why I'm ringing you Mr Smith. I'm new to the account and I'm very concerned about a number of points you raised. I wonder could I meet you just to see how we can put things right?'

He may be quite resolute and hang up, but he might feel he has nothing to lose and agree to see you in view of your reasonable request. If he does the next stage is to *listen*. The amateur would refer to some problems in the past and go on to tell the prospect how good everything is now. Telling is for later. Here we come back to our friends, the emotional and the rational. In complaints and grievances it is the emotional which constitutes the main part of dissatisfaction. The supplier who attacks the rational side of the complaint will seldom win the customer. A minor fault on a piece of equipment that could be very easily rectified may seem no big deal. The rational side of the supplier's defence could seem convincing to him. However, the piece of equipment was a present for somebody very special on a very important occasion and the fact that it did not work completely ruined the occasion and led to tears of frustration. So *listen*.

Take the conference services company salesman:

'Tell me what happened, Mr Smith.'

'I'll tell you what bloody happened! We hired a TV and video equipment from you people for an important conference and it was garbage.'

(The salesman knows it was a simple matter of a small switch not being turned on. As a professional, he does not counter with a smug, simple explanation. This would only exacerbate matters. His job is to defuse the emotion first. He encourages the customer to go on.)

'So when it came to what should have been the high point of the presentation, we cued the video and nothing happened. It entirely spoilt the presentation. It looked unprofessional and made us look fools.'

'Well, we carried on with the flip chart but the damage was done. The mood in the room changed and I know it cost us business.'

The next stage is to *cushion*, that is, to agree, sympathise or identify with the aggrieved:

'What a nightmare. No wonder you were upset. If that happened to me during a presentation, I wouldn't know where to turn.'

This approach helps vent the emotional element of the complaint. There is no point explaining the rational until the emotional factor has subsided. At this stage a better human bond has been formed. With this as a foundation it is possible to build.

When the situation is calmer the rational may be approached: 'I had not realised how bad the day was. I can well understand how you felt. Thank you for explaining it to me. Tell me, do you know what the problem was?'

'It wasn't so much the problem – it was the effect it had!'

'Yes, I can well appreciate that, but for me and my company's benefit do you know where the error lay?'

'Actually it wasn't so much your equipment but the guy who came to set it up just flew through the instructions with one of our junior staff who thought he understood it and your man just went off.'

Here comes the *focus*.

'Oh I see. So it wasn't the equipment, it was the fact that no one took the trouble to show the right people how to use it?'

Had the salesman begun with this, defending his corner, as in 'We checked the equipment out thoroughly, Mr Smith, and there was nothing whatever wrong with it', he would have immediately entered a confrontational situation. The anger or emotion factor, instead of being reduced, would have increased and the salesman would have ended up on the pavement with no chance of ever doing future business.

But now he has the problem in focus, the salesman seeks *agreement*. 'So the equipment was fine but no one took the trouble to show you how to use it properly?'

'Yes.'

Now we have agreement. The final stage is to *overcome*. Another recap might be in order. You could even get a few agreements that the cost was fair, the range of equipment was fine and the delivery was on time. The only objection was the user instruction one. An *overcome* close could be:

'So, Mr Smith, while appreciating the upset you've had, if we could provide the same service but ensure a thorough familiarisation with the equipment, could we do business again?' You might have to throw in a negotiation chip such as a discount, or a free day's loan or even the loan of an operator. It all depends on the value of the customer.

Again we use terms like Objection Handling Skills. The procedure is largely common sense. One way to look at aggrieved customers is like a balloon with a message written on a piece of paper inside it. The air in the balloon represents the emotion and the piece of paper the rational complaint. If you try and get straight to the complaint the balloon will explode. Much wiser to loosen the neck of the balloon. Allow all the emotional air out. When the balloon is deflated it is much easier to extract the rational message and deal with it.

Engineers and repairmen often fall into the trap of attacking the rational. Because they can see things in a logical and practical light, they can tell a customer how simple some fault is to rectify. Possibly the last thing the customer wants to hear is how simple something is to operate, especially as, by implication, it places a degree of fault on the customer. As he is already fuming at the inadequacies of the equipment, it does not help to imply that he is a bit dense as well.

In life, so many arguments gain heat because one party argues from the emotional standpoint and the other from the rational. The husband defends his corner with, 'All you are complaining about is because I didn't make one silly phone call!' The wife considers the spoiled dinner, the uncertainty, the worry, the waiting up, the things she might have done had she known he was not coming, and the lack of consideration.

Negotiation

Negotiation takes place when two (or more) parties with differing perspectives meet to reach a common objective. At Maastricht, twelve European leaders with twelve perspectives sat down to reach a common policy for economic and political union. That is a heavy negotiation.

The essence of negotiation is good 'people skills' plus preparation. When your son says, 'Dad, the car could do with a wash,' you have the beginnings of a negotiation.

'Boss, I want a pay rise!' –

'You can't have one!' is confrontation, not negotiation.

'Dad, if I clean out the garage and wash the car, can you . . .' Here we have the makings of a good negotiator.

In Prospecting (Chapter 4) we looked at preparation and the need for an objective. This fell into three categories: Like to get – Expect to get – Must get.

Trade Union wage bargaining works on this principle. The opening move is often to seek a very substantial increase. A presentation is prepared in detail including several factors such as inflation, productivity, comparisons, unsocial hours, travel distances, length of service, company profits, uncomfortable temperature or conditions, and as many justifications for the increase as possible. A number of bargaining chips will be retained for use when necessary. These could include an agreement to a change in hours or a new shift system, fewer or shorter breaks, raised productivity targets and any other which might apply to that specific industry. Under no circumstances would these chips be thrown into the negotiation pot too early. The negotiation will remain on the *like to get* for as long as possible before dropping a degree or two nearer the *expect to get* figure.

The employers have exactly the same principle of preparation. They *must get* a settlement of under fifteen per cent, say. They *expect to get* one at around nine per cent. They would *like* to get a settlement at five per cent. Their bargaining chips will normally be in the same categories as the employees' but with different parameters. Each of the chips can also have *must*, *expect* and *like* plans. If a chip was increased productivity, the percentage increase could be a separate 'minor goal' negotiation towards achieving the 'major goal' of the wage settlement.

Good Trade Union negotiators would raise the whole issue at a Union meeting, covering all the expectations (or aspirations, to use the popular Union term) and have the bargaining chips agreed in advance.

Preparation includes not just planning your own presentation and bargaining chips but also an anticipation of what demands or moves the other party is likely to make. A boxer will train to the point of exhaustion on his own fitness and skill before a contest. He will also spend some time watching videos or attending fights of his future opponents, as will many other competitive sportsmen. Highly developed match play or fighting techniques are little comfort when retrieving the ball from the back of the net or when you are flat on the canvas.

In sales negotiation the same forethought should apply. What are the buying criteria? Look at a blank sheet of the Closing corridor (Fig. 5) and write down as many demands or objections you can think of against each door. Once you have a clear plan as to which doors need to be closed you are much better prepared to launch into negotiation.

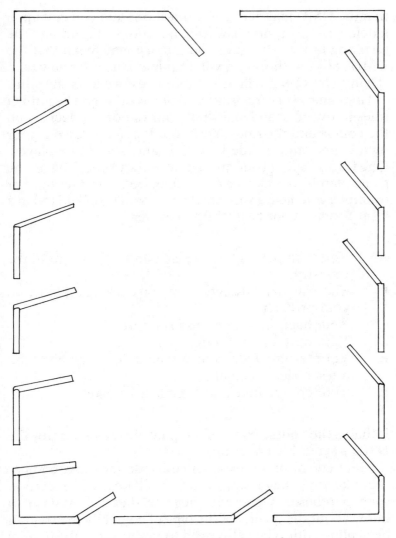

Fig. 5   The Closing Corridor

When selling into major accounts or when in front of committees or any group comprising a DMU (Decision Making Unit), one great fear is loss of control. The risk is

91

that the DMU may start firing questions and you end up in a defensive position answering questions at random. The resulting loss of structure and fluency may mean that the DMU calls the shots and will terminate the interview with 'Thank you very much, don't phone us, we'll phone you.'

This can be very frustrating. You have this golf bag full of sales knowledge and skills but your opponent decides on the course and the rules. You would prefer to lay out your own course and decide how the game should be played. One way of laying your own goalposts and deciding on the game plan is to make a clear and logical introduction. For example, you have a very positive presentation laid out in a clear format. Your best 'clubs' may be:

A. Your company's knowledge and track record in the industry.
B. The excellent design, versatility and durability of your product.
C. Your back-up service and support.
D. Your customer training.
E. Your testimonials from comparable companies who are satisfied customers.
F. Your competitive and flexible lease rates.

If that is the course you wish to play on – lay it out for the DMU in your introduction:

'Gentlemen, in my experience in the industry, companies like yours have expressed several areas of concern in such purchases. Generally they are these: they wish to know about the quality of the type of company they would be dealing with. They also need to know about the quality of the equipment they would be installing along with quality of the service and support they would receive (etc., listing your presentation plan from A to F). Are these the areas of concern that you have?'

The answer is going to be Yes.

'Right gentlemen, I'll run through those areas with you, then if you have any questions please let me have them.'

Depending on your product or service the list can be of whatever length is necessary but the principle is the same – you have control and you can make your presentation your way. Even if the DMU appears to take charge initially by opening with the expressed intention of asking questions, you can still make your opening with a brief prefix: 'Obviously you will have several areas to consider and in my experience in the industry . . .'

In my early days of presentations I made the grave mistake of giving the DMU literature to read as I progressed. The inevitable happened. As soon as any written information was placed in front of the buyer(s), the heads went down and the control and flow of the presentation was lost. Question-hopping began and I had to deal with random questions which sidetracked me from my structure. The result appeared disorganised and unprofessional.

Although ultimately it is the product which the DMU buys, it is the credibility and professionalism of the presenter which they remember. This is very often the deciding factor in a buying decision. Certainly there are very experienced buyers from large institutions who know backwards every comparable product or service, every supplying company and have to hand every current price list. This leads us to conclude that the only deciding factor is price, so we will look first at the price objection. Before we do, let us never assume that price is the only objection. One large corporate vehicle fleet buyer is an example. He had computer records of every vehicle the organisation had ever bought, including model, estate, saloon hatchback or van, mileage, fuel consumption, performance details, price, faults developed and when, service record, difficulty with spares, time off the road, you name it. The organisation's policy was to buy British where possible. The fleet salesman's package for British vehicles won on price but the buyer chose German vehicles because, as he put it, he could live without the hassle.

The Price Objection

All buyers are taught the slow intake of breath technique to accompany the statement, 'You'll have to do better than that!'

The amateur will immediately lop a bit off the price. But remember two rules: *Price is not your only bargaining chip*, and *Do not donate concessions – trade them*.

Firstly, where possible convert cost into value: 'Naturally, with the economic climate the way it is, you will be concerned about value for money. I agree we are not the cheapest in the market but you do have the reassurance of knowing . . .' (here you can list as many benefits as possible along with any special USPs – Unique Selling Points – you may provide).

'Even so, you are still a bit pricey.'

Buyers will seldom ask for a specific discount. They would rather keep fishing to see how far a salesman is prepared to go. Another technique is to ask for an almost preposterous discount as an opening move of negotiation (the 'like to get' card) just to see the salesman's response. Many salespeople can conclude a deal very unhappily, complaining, 'I had to give away all my margin.' But did he have to? Perhaps he capitulated on the buyer's very strong 'like to get' delivery. Maybe the buyer's 'expect to get' bracket was never entered, let alone his 'must get' bracket.

The salesman should stay with his own 'like to get' bracket for as long as possible. When he has to concede a discount he should trade it and not just donate it: 'Because of the quality of our service and support, our margins are very tight indeed. We could not reduce by 10 per cent but I could offer a 5 per cent discount if we could process the order today.'

In the motor trade, there was a very effective negotiation technique. When the street-wise expert came into the showroom (you can always tell him by the way he kicks the tyres), he would ask, 'How much discount can you give me off this one?'

'Well sir, we can give discount on some selected vehicles. But we only do that at the point of sale. Is this the vehicle you wish to buy?'

In other words, we are not going to follow you round the showroom offering discounts on each vehicle whose tyres you kick. When we have gone through a sales process and decided on a vehicle, then we'll talk about discount. Even then discount was not the salesman's only tool. His bargaining chips included free delivery, a full petrol tank, a year's road tax, perhaps a tow bar or any other item or service which at list price could seem more attractive than the net cost to the garage.

Similarly, office equipment salespeople have other bargaining chips such as free consumables – paper, toner, an add-on feature or perhaps another piece of equipment. (The first photocopier I bought was because there was a free telephone answering machine thrown in with the deal. The net cost to the supplier reflected as a percentage of the copier price would have been minimal.)

The ultimate bargaining chip to avoid donating a concession is to ask for the order *now*. Some hilarious stories are told of salesmen who used this method. For instance, the buyer who is quite adamant he will not budge without a 25 per cent discount. The salesman has thrown into the negotiation pot every last bargaining chip, but he knows he can give 25 per cent and still not do too badly. However he is damned if he is going to make it seem like a total submission, so he says, 'A discount of that size is really quite exceptional and my company will never jeopardize the quality of our back-up service. I would need to telephone my office to gain approval for such a substantial discount. If I can gain authorisation, they will quite definitely insist on the order being signed today. So before I pick up the phone, can I have your assurance that we can process the order today?

He does not in fact need approval, so he dials any number, carefully articulating his heavy request. Only when the call is complete does the buyer volunteer, 'Actually, you'll need a 9 to dial out,'.

In fig. 6 there are four negotiation circumstances shown. From the top clockwise they run:

YOU WIN – I WIN
I WIN – YOU LOSE
YOU LOSE – I LOSE
I LOSE – YOU WIN.

Human psychology being what it is, the most desirable for both parties is a WIN – WIN situation. A buyer is not necessarily happy when he asks for concessions.

'Can you throw in a free—?'
'No problem.'
'And can you add a free—?'
'Yes I can do that for you.'
'I'd like the warranty extended.'
'I can arrange that.'
'I'll need a bit off the price.'
'Okay.'

And so on. When the salesman donates concession after concession, the buyer not only wonders just how far he can go but he feels he is not dealing with someone of his peer group. He feels like a pro against an amateur. Instinctively we like a fair fight. We want a conclusion where both parties have their heads up and feel satisfied that a successful negotiation has been settled.

It is not just the emotional satisfaction of a fair bargain but there are practical repercussions. An inexperienced buyer might pay well over the odds for a product or service. He may be contractually obligated and the sale is safe, but the chances of repeat business and a happy client/supplier relationship are minimal when realisation dawns.

Taking fig. 6 and working anti-clockwise the first negotiation circumstances is YOU WIN – I LOSE (You being the buyer, I the seller). The words in that 90 degree sector

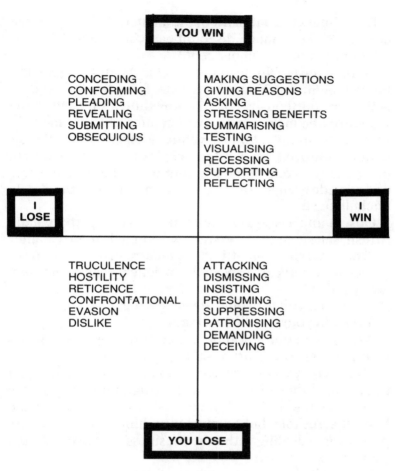

Fig. 6   Negotiation

include conceding and conforming, which we've looked at. Pleading comes next. This is not a tool used by the serious professional, though it is used to some degree by people who should know better.

We all know that the date with the person who played hard to get is much more satisfactory than the pushover.

Revealing is the hallmark of the amateur. 'Right, your list price is £X. How much discount can you give me?'

'On that model – 25 per cent.'

Straight away. No negotiation. Our Asian brothers find this very amusing. You ask Mr Patel for a discount and he will, very courteously, tell you how difficult it is and how little profit he makes. He may then offer a bargaining chip such as if you buy two or give him a bigger order. Rather than be annoyed, he is often delighted to barter. Britain, incidentally, is one of the few countries where fixed prices on a wide range of goods seem to go completely unchallenged.

Obsequiousness was a common behaviour pattern of the British salesman (for reasons we looked at in Chapter 1). Too deferential an attitude is unattractive. The phraseology of yesteryear, especially in letters, can seem very funny indeed:

'Thanking you for your esteemed order.'

'I remain your obedient servant.'

'We express our gratitude in permitting us to submit to your goodselves our proposal for your perusal . . .'

This nonsense is a hangover from the days when being in trade was rather distasteful and being patronised by the gentry was the norm. Granted a salesman wants to make himself agreeable, but he must view himself as a business professional dealing with other business professionals as a peer group.

Early British sales manuals used to advise salesmen to use the buyer's name as often as they can, laugh at his jokes and repeat back anything of value he may say as in, 'Yes Mr Smith, and as you so rightly say yourself, Mr Smith . . .' Dreadful. The American salesman is not obsequious simply because he does not feel in any way beholden or inferior to the buyer. He has never been conditioned by the peculiarly British malaise of 'I know my place'.

The I LOSE – YOU LOSE situation is where no sale takes place. The buyer loses a product or service which could have benefited him and the salesman loses an order. Sometimes this can be caused by a simple clash of personalities. We all know situations where a buyer will continue to do business with a certain company but refuses point-blank to deal with a certain salesman. I clearly remember an excellent client/supplier relationship that was nearly ruined by a sales manager accompanying one of his salesmen on a call. The seller and buyer had quite a long-term relationship. They liked and trusted each other and generally got on very well together. The sales manager – perhaps being over-eager or wishing to impress his salesman – tried to close for an order that was not quite ready to drop. The meeting turned a little nasty with an element of hostility and truculence entering the exchange.

Later the buyer phoned the seller and said 'Listen George, we get on fine and I'll continue to do business with you, but don't ever bring that (*expletive deleted*) with you again.'

Confrontation can develop through talking when you should be listening, assuming, misinterpretation, telling the buyer what you want to sell without understanding his needs, or some form of ignorance whether of your own product or the industry into which you are selling. Other confrontation can be so basic as to be insurmountable. The Glaswegian salesman wearing a Celtic tie who sees in the buyer's office corner masonic regalia and a Rangers scarf might be wise to re-appoint and send a colleague. Who knows, the chemistry might be one of mutual respect and genuine human liking.

Reticence on the part of the buyer may indicate some hidden objection or hostility. The wise salesman would avoid any 'telling' and opt for some open probes to ensure the foundation for any further negotiation was sound.

Evasion generally occurs in one specific area – price.

'Okay, how much is this going to cost me?'

None of us welcome the question, especially when we have not finished making a thorough presentation of the many benefits. Salesmen reply with some terrible answers: 'I'd rather not talk about price just yet, Mr Smith' or 'I'll come to that in a moment' or 'If you'll just hold on till I've finished this . . .'

In essence what the salesman is saying is quite logical and even reasonable. He wants to make quite clear that he has established the correct needs. He then wants to ensure that the prospect appreciates fully how the product would meet the needs, then he will go on to justify his price. However, the buyer sees it differently and the essence of good negotiation is to understand the other party's viewpoint. The buyer believes the salesman is afraid of price. Why? Is it a bit of a con? Doubts begin to gather. The more the salesman carries on the more the buyer believes the salesman is being evasive. The danger is that, even if the salesman manages to side-step price, the buyer may stop listening and become preoccupied with the issue.

When showing a prospect round a health club the prospect would often ask, 'How much is it?' Any evasion resulted in the prospect switching off and some of the more powerful aspects of the show-round were lost.

When asked about price when you are not quite ready to cover it, always acknowledge the question: 'Okay, Mr Brown, you want to get full details of prices, payment plans and lease rates, yes?'

Whether you go on to do just that is not vital. What is vital is that you have stopped, listened and acknowledged the request for information.

You now have a few options. You could say 'Fine. I was just coming to that. Would you prefer me to finish with just a couple more details, then I'll go over the pricing structure in full, or do you want me to skip straight on to the pricing policy?'

The main strength of this is that you have acceded to his request. You have shown yourself perfectly willing to go directly to the answer to his question and you have avoided the serious psychological barrier associated with evasion.

Human nature may well permit, 'Finish your point but I am concerned about cost', and here is an opportunity for feel – felt – found harmony: 'I quite understand how you *feel* Mr Brown . . .'

Another option is to give a rough estimate or ballpark figure. Again, acknowledge immediately the question: 'Right, Mr Brown, obviously you want a comprehensive breakdown of all the costs involved. I'll go over the complete price list with you. Can I give you a rough estimate just now?'

'Okay.'

'It depends on the package, but we are not talking of more than a few pounds a day.'

The fact it costs £10,000 over a five-year lease can wait.

The psychological advantage is that you have not evaded but involved the buyer. You have made him part of the decision-making process. The question 'Which shall I do?' recognises his importance in the exchange. He is not being talked *at*. His request for price information may not even be an anxiety but simply a wish to assert himself in what he considers to be too much of a one-sided exchange. By acknowledging his query and requesting his view you may redress the balance and gain the time needed to finish your presentation.

The I LOSE – YOU LOSE situation could occur over cost. I lose the sale and the buyer loses the product purely because he has not got the finance. Where this situation occurs because of poor skills with product, presentation or people, then honest self-analysis is essential.

One final tip concerning objections is *never answer a statement with a statement*.

'Your products have a very bad reputation.'

'No they haven't.'

The salesman could well be correct. He may even feel outraged at such a suggestion but they have just touched gloves. The bell has gone, so let the boxing commence:

'Our York office has one and it never works' (left hook).

'I installed that and it was perfect' (right cross).

Let us try again, this time answering a statement with a question.

'Your products stink.'

'Oh. What makes you say that?'

'Our York office . . .' etc.

'That's interesting. Tell me about that.'

And so on, letting all the air out of the balloon, before making any statement whatever. That type of reasonable and non-confrontational objection handling will lead us to a situation of I WIN – YOU WIN.

The I WIN – YOU LOSE situation is where the salesman may actually gain the sale but to the detriment of the customer. This sector covers unprofessional conduct such as deceiving, suppressing, insisting and dismissing. Where ongoing customer/client relationships are desirable, these defects are the kiss of death. In a one-off 'gold-Rolex-in-the-pub' sale the actual objective of the sale is almost certainly an I WIN – YOU LOSE exercise. The backstreet garage which tells you that the car had 'one careful owner' may not be concerned about repeat business. Unfortunately I WIN – YOU LOSE tactics are sometimes used by sales people who could seek repeat business or referrals but their pursuit of the short-term gain is too great for the long-term interest. This is normally not the fault of the company but of the individual who wants his reward now and is not too sure where he will be in the future. It makes life more difficult for our profession as a whole. When you hear, 'The salesman who sold me this said it would—' alarm bells should ring. You now know you will have to close the You door, the Company door and the Product door very firmly.

In this context, there is sometimes a temptation to score with, 'Who sold you this, then?' It really does not help to imply that the prospect has been sold a pup and that he is a bigger fool than he already felt he was. Far better to be professionally analytical and sympathise with, 'Perhaps ABC Ltd did not fully appreciate your needs at the time.'

This is a more dignified approach and is an excellent introduction to justify your own more thorough probing exercise. Also, if a buyer criticises an existing product or service provided by a competitor, don't join in. If you do join in with a gloating comment to the effect that you had always heard they were rubbish, not only do you detract form your own dignity but you may even prompt the buyer to reflect on some redeeming features. It is wiser to offer a token defence of your competitor such as 'I'm surprised to hear that. They have quite a good reputation in the market.'

Human nature being what it is, as you have offered a token defence of the competitor, the buyer may step up his attack: 'Good reputation? Well let me tell you . . .' He'll then proceed to blacken the picture for you.

Try this little test of psychology for yourself. The next time someone tells you they have been to a restaurant or holiday resort (or bought a product) that was awful, just say you had a friend who went there and who said it was great. However black the picture was before your comment, it will be substantially blacker after it.

Turning to I WIN – YOU WIN, the first recommendation is making suggestions: 'What if . . .?', 'How about . . .?' are excellent tools in negotiation. The Maastricht Treaty was saved from possible breakdown by a 'What if Britain is excluded from the social legislation element?' An unhappy compromise where Britain is left to make its own arrangements with the other eleven states, but a compromise nonetheless.

The enemy of negotiation is the brick wall. When parties become entrenched in their views and will not budge, negotiation fails. The banqueting manager: 'What if we provide the wine from list A but the food from list B?' The machinery salesman: 'What if we remove your old machine, thoroughly refurbish it and install it in your new factory and we install the new machine here?'

Giving reasons: Seemingly casual comments like, 'Your machine is quite large, isn't it', should not be met with, 'It is a bit.' Better to say, 'Actually for the amount of work it will achieve, it is really very compact.'

'It doesn't look much.' – 'I understand your comment. With the advanced technology we have developed this machine will actually achieve twice the throughput of machines three times its size.'

Similarly with support statements. If your product receives a compliment – use it.

'It certainly looks nice.'

The amateur would smile, 'Yes it does, doesn't it.' The pro says, 'Our company has its own research and development division which means the design is excellent. But it not only looks good, it is superbly engineered.'

'The paintwork has a good finish.' – 'It should do, Mr Smith. After total immersion protection treatment, it receives twenty-six coats of high durability paint.'

'Your copy quality is very good.' – 'I though you'd be impressed. You are looking at advanced laser technology which not only provides a flawless copy but continues to provide it consistently, copy after copy.'

Asking and summarising, in other words seeking confirmation and clarification throughout a sales presentation or negotiation, is essential. It makes summarising so much easier – not necessarily the main summary at the end but it will assist mini-summaries en route to the end.

Visualising and stressing benefits: No holiday brochure would think of showing a picture of Gatwick Airport with thousands of miserable, waiting passengers. Nor would it show blistered Brummies applying calamine lotion in the shade. Everyone is golden brown and smiling happily by an uncrowded pool. Estate agents also have an interesting approach to presentation. 'A stone's throw from the shops' and 'public transport a few steps from the door' might apply to David and Goliath respectively.

Painting pictures is effective: 'So the vending machine would fit neatly in that corner. That would be perfect. You could get rid of all that mess by the kettle. There is easy access from each room and all the delays and inconvenience would be eliminated so you have a clean, efficient machine for instant supply and happy staff.'

Even intangibles like insurance can involve visualising. The transaction may seem rather cold and mercenary, it needs a little more warmth: 'Once you are under cover it will be a weight off your shoulders. You can sleep peacefully at night knowing that . . .'

Recessing is a negotiation tool which does not normally enter the sales interview. It is regularly used in large-scale negotiation where things get bogged down or tempers begin to flare. The alert negotiator will suggest a break for coffee or, to use that ghastly modern term, a 'bio' break. (Why 'bio' for heaven's sake? If people want to use the lavatory, do they need to be told the purpose of the break!) A recess can be valuable in allowing a little time to gather thoughts, reflect and compose.

It can be used in some sales situations. In domestic sales, such as replacement windows, when a salesman finds a sticking point, he may ask to use the bathroom. He can then return to approach the obstacle from a different angle or conduct a mini-summary of what was agreed so far.

7

CLOSING

You've reached the stage to close. You've blocked all the more important doors. The buyer feels happy with you. He is aware of all the benefits of your product or service.

Remember, a benefit is only a benefit when it meets an expressed need of the buyer. John Cleese illustrates this perfectly in one of his training videos. He is running a stall selling water. A prospect approaches with his wife. Cleese tells him about the wonderful uses of water – for brushing teeth, washing, watering the garden, keeping goldfish and so on. The prospect seems uninterested and leaves. The wife asks her husband, 'Not interested then, dear?'

'No. I was looking for something to drink.'

The buyer likes the feel of your company and the support it provides. Finally you have justified your price. You have reached the point where there really is nothing left to say. So it is time for the close.

Teaching someone to close is difficult. Mostly the more experienced teach how they would do it. You'll hear the older salesmen tell the novice, 'You should have closed him there.' Maybe. Closing is a very personal issue. If you simply do not feel right or you are just blindly following what someone else has advised, it can be very risky. Rather like someone else's chat-up line at a party. He gets away with it while you get your face slapped.

We looked earlier at the mystique which surrounds the question of closing. The reason for it is because there is no answer. As with the Magic Weight Loss Diet it does not exist. Gullible slimmers flock to worship at the shrine of the latest One True Slimming Aid only to find it to be as big a disappointment as the last one. Salespeople in general are more streetwise and know there is no hypnotic combination of words to render the buyer incapable of saying 'No'. We know it is a blending of what you feel happy saying, the situation and the person to whom you are selling.

One salesman I accompanied took me to see a customer. When we breezed in, the buyer said, 'What do you want, you big ugly bugger?'

'The salesman replied, 'I'll tell you what I want. I want an order. I want it now and I want a big one so I don't have to come back and see you again too soon.'

He got his order. Now, if you were to put that in a sales training manual, the Nigels, Tarquins and Carolines of the marketing world would be horrified. But that salesman closed the buyer with an ease and fluency which were absolutely perfect for the given situation. The exchanged insults gave a clear signal of a very good relationship.

Although all closes come under one of several categories, the words and manner used are as variable as the types of people and situations we meet.

One salesperson uses precisely the same closing technique as another, yet one gains the sale and the other ends up being shown the door or involved in a lengthy objection-handling exercise. The difference can be that one salesman has earned the right to close, whereas the other has left a few doors ajar or even wide open. Because we can be reluctant to undergo honest self-analysis and admit fault in the thoroughness of our door closing, we often blame the close at the end.

Granted some closing phrases are clearly better than others but often the accolade, 'He's a brilliant closer', can mean that the man is more thorough, consequently his timing is excellent. Another attribute for a brilliant closer is that he is not afraid to ask for the order when he considers the time ripe. If the mood is right he may even close early. 'Mr Smith, there really is no doubt that this is the system for you. Shall we just go ahead and do the paperwork?' Such a positive reassurance may be just what was needed to get the order, without further selling (or over-selling). Even if Mr Smith is not quite ready, at least he will articulate whatever remaining concerns he has, giving the salesman the opportunity to handle those specific points.

A further attribute of a brilliant closer is that buyers just feel comfortable with him. As in the Alan Whicker mould, he is quiet, professional, thorough and knowledgeable. The beauty of selling *you* is that automatically buyers are less wary of your product or your company. The perfect sale is where the salesman completes the entire door-closing exercise without consciously selling and the process is so natural the buyer is not conscious of being sold to.

So to conclude that a brilliant closer is someone with a few good punch-lines is to fail to understand the psychology of selling. In every presentation the content is important but it is the delivery which decides the reaction. To read the content of a Frankie Howerd or Tommy Cooper script would not be at all funny – but what a delivery! What can be worse than listening to someone who has been to see a 'really funny show'. He kills himself with laughter as he recalls each sketch and retells you some 'hilarious' jokes. Your pained smile becomes fainter at each successive story. He has had the benefit of both content and delivery. You, alas, are given only the content.

Assuming you have earned the right to close, let us have a look at some general principles. Ask fifty salespeople what they actually say at the close and you could get fifty different answers. Generally we dislike some words like 'sign' or 'contract'. We prefer phrases like 'okay the paperwork'. Some prefer to avoid the direct close altogether and choose to close on a minor issue, such as, 'When do you want it delivered?' (We'll take a look at them all in a moment.)

This is a good point to stress one very useful rule: *Decide in advance what you are going to say.* If you get to the end of a sale, you know you must close. You've put in quite a lot of work. The size of your wage cheque depends on the outcome; so does your self-esteem and your standing in the eyes of your colleagues. You can become tense. Because you have not decided in advance what you are going to close with, you find ten different phrases spinning in your mind. You go for it. Unfortunately two or three closing phrases spring to your lips simultaneously and out comes a question which can range from the not-quite-right to gobbledegook. A display of uncertainty or lack of confidence could jeopardize the sale. Even if the content of your closing phrase is quite banal, as long as it suits you and you feel comfortable with it, that's fine.

The direct close

As the name suggests, you simply ask for the order.

'Can we go ahead?' or 'Shall we complete the paperwork?' or 'Can I have your approval on the order form?'

It is more effective to prefix the direct close with a confident, 'Well, as you seem quite happy with everything, can we . . .?' or 'If you have no further questions, shall we . . .?'

One risk with the direct close is that it is a closed question and even when well delivered it could invite a 'No.' A stronger version is:

The assumptive close

You really must earn the right to close with this. You are satisfied that you have closed all the doors so you confidently conclude with: 'Right. This is definitely the correct system for you. Let's go and do the paperwork', or prefix the close with a brief summary: 'So you're quite happy with A, with B, with C, etc. Fine. Let's go and do the paperwork.'

The word 'let's' is very powerful. It is particularly effective with indecisive buyers.

As humans we respond to decisive people. People who make decisions or are 'born leaders' are respected. We all know situations where, as a couple or a group, you are undecided what to do and someone says: 'I know – let's go to . . .' We respond favourably (even if the idea is not particularly good).

Only when we have not earned the right to close can the assumptive close be unwise. The shop assistant who says, 'Shall I wrap it up for you?' before you are ready to buy, merits our dislike.

Some people are just naturally weak or afraid of making a commitment. The professional salesperson is the one who can minimise this fear and makes the buying decision as easy as possible.

A major indirect benefit of the assumptive close is that it can pinpoint an objection. The buyer is far from being Mr Indecisive. You close him with, 'Well, as you seem quite happy with everything, let's go ahead and do the paperwork.' Either he will comply and the sale is made or he must respond with a clear objection. If he has a clear objection you have a chance to handle it. It is the weak and vague 'I'd like to think about it' objection which gives us problems.

Closing on a minor (or secondary) issue

Rather than ask for the order directly (or assume you are getting it), you can close on a minor issue:

'When would you like it delivered?'

'Do you want it with tow bar or without?' (see also Alternative Close).

110

When closing on a minor issue, you will probably still need to finish with a direct or assumptive close: 'With a tow bar, fine – let's go and do the paperwork'.

The benefit of the minor issue close is that it softens the rather confrontational 'will you buy or will you not buy' situation. Instead it focuses on a lesser issue such as delivery date, colour, payment method or add-on features. Closing on a minor issue can also be used as a trial close.

The trial close

This can be used at almost any stage. It is used to test for buying signals. In a probing interview or half way through a demonstration, you stop and reflect: 'Incidentally, Mr Smith, when were you thinking of installation?'

If done coolly it can evince a very welcome and positive response. 'We must have it installed by . . .'

Or it can provide a new avenue to probe. For example, if the response was: 'We haven't decided yet but it will be either January or March', you have a new and interesting direction to probe, i.e. 'Oh, why is that?'

Having used a trial close and gained a strong buying signal, e.g. 'It must come out of this year's budget', don't make the mistake of abandoning the rest of the sale. Carry on professionally shutting any remaining doors. There is nothing to stop you throwing in another trial close as you go on: 'Where exactly are you thinking of siting the equipment?' or 'Regarding staff training – will you want them all trained together or just a few at a time?'

Each trial close cements in the buyer's mind that the decision is made. So when you come to shut that final door for the order, the assumptive close may be used quite naturally and with a high degree of confidence.

The alternative close

The alternative close is almost indistinguishable from closing on a minor issue. The strength of both is that each avoids the pitfalls of a Yes or No showdown. So rather than create an element of possible tension with 'Can I have your order?' (a direct close), the alternative close simply asks which alternative the buyer would prefer. It is used very effectively where the choices are wide as in the motor trade or in computer installations. Health club memberships sales were closed with, 'Do you want the one-year membership, the popular two-year or the super economy five-year membership?' The question was not, 'Are you joining or not?'

'The red one or the blue one?'; 'Cash or cheque?'; 'Three-year lease agreement or five-year?' – all are alternative closes. (They would also fall under the category of closing on a minor issue.) In retail sales there has been a general trend towards removing the smaller or cheaper alternatives. When was the last time you saw toilet rolls or kitchen paper towels sold in ones, or single tins of beer, or small packets of soap powder? You've closed yourself by being in the supermarket, now the sale is: Do you want the big one or the very big one?

The Winston Churchill close

Also known as the Benjamin Franklin close, the George Washington close, the Duke of Wellington close and the 'T' close. No doubt in France it is known as the Charles de Gaulle close. No book on sales is complete without this specimen. Used by every theoretician but very seldom used by salesmen in the field. Oddly, every salesman knows somebody who has used it but no one has ever used it himself.

It is quite old-fashioned now and if done badly can be

patronising and offensive. Sometimes used in domestic sales but very rare in corporate selling. The principle is simple. A prospective buyer is being particularly indecisive. You are satisfied you have closed all the doors. You ask to buy. You handle a couple of objections. You close again. No response – he strokes chin. He hums and haws. You try the assumptive close: 'Let's go and do the paperwork.' He says, 'Well, I'm not really too sure . . .' Looks like a job for Winston Churchill. (Given time, it may even be known as the Margaret Thatcher close. Remember, you read it here first.)

You explain that whenever Winston Churchill (or whatever historic figure seems appropriate) had to make an important decision he took a blank sheet of paper and drew on it a large T. He listed all the reasons for the decision on one side of the T and the against factors on the other side. You then proceed to use the method with, 'Let's try it.' You write down all the benefits of your product or service. Tangible benefits will come quickly but add in a few intangibles as well such as 'peace of mind' or 'reliable back-up service'. Where possible, always get the cost factor on the *For* side.

Having drawn up a comprehensive list on the *For* side you summarise with: 'That looks a pretty strong case to go ahead. Let's see what is against the purchase.'

The prospect is then very much left on his own to find reasons not to buy. Invariably the *For* list will be considerably longer than the *Against*. The very visual impact of a long list for and a short list against is used to close the sale with an assumptive close: 'Looks pretty conclusive, doesn't it – let's do the paperwork.'

In the, quite literally, thousands of health clubs sales I was involved in, I only remember the T close being used three or four times. I used it once with two very indecisive lady prospects in Glasgow. I wrote down a long column of health and appearance benefits; slim waist, firm hips, good bust-line, better skin, better circulation, improved posture and so on. I had probably twenty benefits on one side and on the *Against* side were two factors – sacrifice of two hours a week and the cost of a few games of bingo. Not only was it effective as a visual selling tool but it also helped to isolate any objection. The women had seen attending the club as a sacrifice or a grind. To counteract this I impressed them that an evening in the gym was fun and they would meet lots of like-minded women who really enjoyed the chat and the spirit of the evening. Thus assured the only remaining objection was cost, which when compared with an evening in the pub or at the bingo hall, was soon overcome; both signed on the dotted line.

If cost is on the *Against* side, there is often a saving on the *For* side which can overcome it. For example, in the health club sale, the cost of the membership could easily be offset by the cutting down on junk food, alcohol or cigarettes. Likewise in a replacement window sale the heat-loss factor or the enhanced value of the house could justify the investment. With Cable TV, the saving on video rentals; office equipment, the saving on man hours.

The T close does have its risks. It can appear a bit laborious and come across as manipulative if not done well. The verbal equivalent is used all the time and works very well indeed. It is known as:

The process-of-elimination close

The circumstances are the same. The prospect is indecisive. You've covered everything and closed a couple of times with no firm response. So rather than write down a *For* list, you just tick off the *Fors* on your fingers:

'You want to think about it? Okay Mr Smith, that is part of my job, to help you in any way I can. Now the car is within your price bracket' – 'Yes.'

'You agree the mileage and condition of the car is fine?' – 'Yes.'

'You're happy with the paint work?' – 'Yes.'

'It has four new tyres, which is what you wanted?' – 'Yes.'

'We're giving you a year's road tax, okay?' – 'Yes.'

The process of elimination goes on, finishing with a direct close: 'So, there's really nothing else to think about. Can we go ahead with the paperwork?' Or the more assumptive: 'Unless there is something I've missed, this is definitely your car. Let's go and do the paperwork.'

The process of elimination is sometimes called climbing the Yes ladder. The principle is to have the buyer make a series of affirmative responses. You like this – Yes. You like that – Yes. So when the final question is asked, 'Can we go ahead and do the paperwork?' it is harder to break the pattern and inject a negative. However, if the buyer does conclude with a negative, he really must offer some clear objection to justify it. When given a clear objection, the salesman at least has something to get his teeth into.

There is nothing so frustrating for a salesman as the vague, 'I want to think about it.' Or 'Leave it with me', or 'I'll get back to you in a couple of days.'

You will never overcome every objection, but a professional salesperson should at least isolate the objection. As a sales manager, whenever one of my sales staff said 'He wants to think about it', I always asked what it was precisely that the prospect wanted to think about. Whenever a salesperson could not answer the question, I made the point that the reason he or she did not know was because they did not ask! They did not isolate the objection. A good isolating exercise would run something like this:

'Most interesting but I'll need to think about it.'

'Yes, I can see you are interested, Mr Smith. What particularly did you want to think about?'

'I just want to consider the whole package and give it some thought.'

'I see. Naturally any purchase of this kind has to be assessed fully and as I am a widget specialist it is part of my job to ensure you are given all the information you need. Just to clarify my own thinking, you're quite happy with the capacity of the machine?'

'Yes, that seems fine.'

'And delivery and service are in line with what you want?'

'Yes.'

And so on. You won't always reach a firm objection but you will be much more successful than just accepting a vague 'think about it' objection.

If you have to accept 'Give me a couple of days and I'll get back to you', try and pin it down:

'Okay Mr Smith, today's Monday, so that'll be Wednesday. Will you ring me or would you prefer me to ring you? . . . You'll ring me. Right. Well, I want to ensure I'm in the office to take your call. Would that be morning or afternoon? . . . Afternoon, fine. I'll put that in my diary now to expect your call on Wednesday afternoon.'

Sure, he may not ring you but it will always prove much more effective than leaving the sale with a vague promise of getting back to you 'in a couple of days'.

The physical action close

This is first cousin to the assumptive close. You have shown your motor car, office equipment system, glossy pictures of the latest pine kitchen or whatever your product or service might be. You ask for the order. Veteran salesmen will tell you their own 'silence' story. They tend to exaggerate but you'll often hear, 'We stood there facing each other, not saying a word for a full five minutes!' or 'I asked him to buy, and I shut up. He looked at me for two minutes solid. Then he picked up the contract and read every word of it for – I kid you not – fifteen minutes.' There is always a basis of truth in these stories. It probably did quite genuinely feel like five or fifteen minutes but in fact

116

the eyeballing lasted ten seconds and the contract was read in two minutes. Because salesmen know the old adage, The First to Speak Loses, these 'silence' stories tend to become embellished.

There are occasions when Mr Indecisive has hummed and hawed for a little too long. Some physical action can be very effective. Pull out a chair saying, 'Right Mr Smith, take a seat.' Take out your pen. 'Now I'll need a few details from you . . .' With the agreement in hand, 'If you have your cheque book with you I can get your banking details for the lease arrangement.'

Even the act of taking your hands from your sides and clasping them together has a note of finality about it. Do this and nod your head towards a seating area or coffee machine, 'Let's get a cup of coffee and do the paperwork. What do you take in your coffee?' The 'What do you take in your coffee?' is quite clever because it cushions the issue of the paperwork. It could be described as an assumptive close with closing on a minor issue. Another example might be, 'Can we go ahead with the paperwork? Incidentally, when did you want delivery?' By giving an affirmative response to the minor issue the buyer tacitly accepts the major issue as well.

With physical action, the involvement of a third party can be effective. 'Susan, could you bring Mr Smith and me a cup of coffee while we complete this paperwork?' If Mr Smith is going to give you an objection, it would have to come out at this juncture.

The order form blank close

This close is first cousin to the assumptive and full brother to the physical action. You have done as thorough a job as you can but still no commitment from the buyer. Your objective is to get some ink on the agreement. The more you can fill in and the more detail the buyer can give you the more concrete the sale becomes. 'Now the full company name is ... and the address is ... and the post code ...' If the buyer is going to stop you, it should happen as pen touches paper.

It goes without saying that if you have not earned the right to close and left a few areas uncovered, you could alienate the buyer by attempting this most presumptuous of closes.

The reverse angle close

Like the T Close, no sales manual is complete without this gem, also known as the Half Nelson. The principle is this. The buyer asks, 'Will it do—?' and the response is to counterpunch or reverse the angle with, 'Will you buy it if it does?' As a close it is clumsy and confrontational but the principal is useful during negotiation. If a buyer asks if your machine will be able to do some function, rather than just saying 'Yes', the professional knows that questions are expressions of interest. The amateur sees questions as hostile or as a nuisance or simply as questions. The professional's ears prick up at a question. He wants to know why the buyer asks, why is that important to him and what benefits could he derive from it. The salesman can then do a mini-reverse angle: 'So any machines you install will have to be able to do that, yes?' You have then obtained a close. I prefer the term 'naildown' for all the intermediate closes on the way to the final close. Naildowns are very valuable. When you have good, clear naildowns or commitments, it makes the presentation of the summary very positive and professional.

If a buyer asked, 'Does your vending machine produce cold drinks?' the old-fashioned hard sell response would be on the lines of 'Will you buy one if it does?' Much better to probe; how important is that; what ratio of hot to cold do you think there would be; what flavours would be most

118

popular; would it change seasonally; and so on. Gain the commitment or naildown which is so useful later for the close, but it is unwise to use the naildown as an opportunity to ask for the order.

The sympathy close

This close can be used either with a degree of dignity or with none at all. Either way it is not very professional. It was more common in the early days of door-to-door encyclopedia, sewing machine and vacuum cleaner salesmen. It still rears its unpretty head in some domestic sales. It was, and still can be, used when a sale appeared to be lost or was very finely in the balance. The salesman would use a sob story about a Christmas bonus to buy presents for the kids or even his job being on the line if certain quotas were not met. (There is a very funny scene in the movie *The Tin Men* where the latter example was used.)

If used with a degree of dignity it can be acceptable as in: 'Mr Smith, I'll be frank with you. There is a company competition running at present. It ends this week. If you place your order today, I qualify for a holiday for two in Greece. I appreciate you wanting to think about it but rather than postpone the decision, can I have the order today?'

That way, you have not demeaned yourself. You have been professional but injected a not unreasonable sympathy close. At worst it could isolate an objection with, 'I'm sorry I can't give you the order today because . . .'

Impending event close

Retail outlets use this all the time: *Closing Down Sale; Clearance Sale – Everything Must Go; Last Few Days; Must End Friday.* In professional direct selling we can use a price increase, an introductory offer, end of line, beating a VAT increase or almost any impending event. Try to be more credible than some high street shops who have been running Special Clearance Sales for years.

The puppy dog close

The origin of the name is quite self-explanatory. The prospective buyer cannot decide whether to buy the puppy or not. The pet shop owner suggests taking it home for a couple of days to see how the family get on with it. The shop owner calls a couple of days later to collect the puppy. Result? Pretty obvious. Mail order companies use this close. 'Try it in the comfort of your own home. If not delighted . . . full refund.' Even people who are less than delighted often can't be bothered to return the goods.

The close is popular in the office equipment industry. A brand new state-of-the-art word processor or copier working alongside old-fashioned equipment makes the purchase all the more attractive.

A word of caution. The amateur may see this close as a soft option. The professional does not donate concessions, he trades them. If the prospective buyer wants five days, the pro gives him three. If he's asked for three he gives two. Most importantly, he pre-closes: 'Yes Mr Smith, I think I can arrange to let you have the machine for a few days. However, it would be on the understanding that providing the machine does meet your requirements, we can have your order.'

The lost sale close

If you know why you lost the sale, fine, leave politely. On occasion you may be shown the door not knowing precisely why you have lost the sale. The lost sale close is really

120

the last shot in your locker. You have closed and handled objections to the point where the exchange could become confrontational. All in vain. Close up your briefcase, shake the buyer's hand and proceed to the door. On the threshold you turn back to the buyer with, 'Just before I go Mr Smith, could I ask your advice on something?'

Disarmed at your request for help (and maybe your promise to go), he agrees, and you continue.

'It's just that I was really pretty certain that you were happy with everything. I quite respect your decision to purchase elsewhere but when I go back to my manager, he will ask me for my order form. When I tell him I haven't got the order, he will ask why. Frankly, I am not sure what to tell him. Perhaps you could help me here. I am always learning, so any advice you could give me would be appreciated.'

The logic is simple. You have nothing to lose. The buyer may come out with some obscure objection which you might be able to overcome. On the other hand there may even be some relatively simple objection, perhaps a misunderstanding over specification or pricing. (One classic springs to mind, where the buyer took the quarterly lease rates to be monthly ones.)

The response may even be painful involving personal or company criticism but you can never find a solution until you understand the problem.

In the bad old days when selling was at its least professional, the most common complaint was about high pressure selling. Truly professional selling should be about reducing pressure, covering thoroughly the three stages of a sale; Establish the need – Prove you can meet the need – Justify your price. When done with care and professionalism the pressure is minimal. High pressure selling occurs when the salesperson closes too hard or too early or when he tries to push goods or services which are clearly at variance with the buyer's needs. There will always be a degree of pressure or tension as the sale nears the close, so the more relaxing and smoothly the close can be presented the better.

Humour can be a great help. A salesman friend of mine with an attractive sense of humour has used what he called the ink close. It went something like this:

'Tell me, John, what colour ink do you have in your pen?'

'Ink? Well actually it's blue. Why?'

'Could I see a sample of it on this dotted line?'

Delivered with a smile, it seemed to have the desired effect. Not universally recommended but if it works for you, fine. We return to the general principle of presentation. Even relatively poor content which comes across naturally in a relaxed way is better than 'clever' closing techniques which you are not happy with.

After-sales procedure

Anyone who has ever closed a sale knows the feeling of satisfaction, even elation, that comes with a signed agreement. The tendency is to grab the document and rush back to the office. No intelligent salesman would do this, but your demeanour and body language may give clues to your inclinations. This can make the buyer uneasy.

You have been very attentive to the buyer as the sale progressed. You listened carefully and showed concern towards his needs. Then, before the ink is dry, your manner changes. You could damage the special inter-personal relationship which is the foundation stone on which most sales are built.

When the document is signed, push it casually to one side and talk about the acquisition – delivery dates, siting, training or just recap some of the benefits. Compare diaries and arrange a return visit. Do not allow the contract to be the focal point; it should appear almost incidental to the main business of looking after the customer. If the selling process were a line on a graph, the close should not appear as a steep peak but more a continuation of a steady horizontal line. If the job is done properly there should be no display of tension, excitement or fear.

8

WRITING A PROPOSAL

The salesman returns to his office. 'How did you get on?' he is asked. 'Guy just would not sign. Says he must have a proposal in writing!' The salesman slaps his briefcase on his desk and slumps down like a loser.

Traditionally in direct selling we have looked upon proposal writing as a form of failure. Schooled in the more aggressive sales techniques we feel we should have 'closed him then and there'. There is some justification in this. The proposal can be a soft option. Rather than go through a solid objection handling and closing exercise, it may be the course of least resistance to put a proposal in the post. On the other hand it may be absolutely essential, as in major account selling.

Honest self-analysis is important here. If there genuinely is no other way to obtain the order than through the submission of a proposal, fine, let's do one and do it properly.

A strange transformation can come over some salesmen when they have to submit a proposal. They take off their salesman hat and put on their accountant hat. All the enthusiastic and forceful presentation of benefits is forgotten. All the interest in and empathy with the buyer is omitted. In fact all the human rapport, perhaps built up over several visits, is laid aside. Instead we submit a document full of dull, lifeless, factual information.

> To supplying one XJK1800 widget with decarbonised sprocket and 8 mm flange. Finish in Pantone 1453 with opaque slurge panel.
>
> All for £18,000 plus VAT

Then we finish with some choice waffle-speak (as seen in Mailshots in chapter 4). 'If you have any further queries in this matter do not hesitate to contact the writer in the first instance . . . assuring you of our best intentions . . . awaiting your esteemed order . . .'

I suspect this murder of the English language is historic. Probably in every office there is a model proposal which has been there since some latter-day Bob Cratchit first scratched his quill across the parchment. Every subsequent proposal has been based upon the original. But worse, with the advent of word processors, much of this clumsy and archaic verbiage has become stored in memory banks throughout the land.

However, let us not dwell on the niceties of English usage. The main issue is that the proposal is essentially a sales letter. So how should it read? The first base is to consider our old friend Kipling and his 'six serving men' – Who, What, Why, Where, When and How. The 'six' can be used in many analytical situations. When selling a sales training consultancy service, I used them all the time. When a prospect expressed an interest in sales training but could not be too precise, they always got results. Why do you want training? What is the objective? What is the current dissatisfaction? Who are the staff concerned? Where is the training to take place, (in-house, hotel, etc). When? Why then? How many? How long?

Not only are the 'six' useful in any problem-solving exercise but it looks extremely professional when they are fired at the prospect. So much so that buyers have often commented, 'you seem to have covered everything very thoroughly'.

So let us use the 'six' in proposal presentation.

> *Why do they need a proposal?*
> *What is the objective of this proposal?*
> *Who else is submitting proposals?*
> *Who is the proposal for?*
> *Where is the proposal to be sent? (Branch office, HO?)*
> *When has it to be in by? When will a decision be made?*
> *When should I follow up a proposal?*
> *How many people in the DMU and what are their buying criteria?*

These are the base questions. Additional questions could be asked but let us work on the base. Firstly – Why do they need a proposal? Let's assume that your contact needs it to present to a committee or board. It is important to know this. You may have done a first-class sales job on your contact. He may even be in favour of you, your product and your company. However, it is unlikely that your contact will be able to (or have the opportunity to) convey to his DMU some of the enthusiasm and the benefits of your presentation. It is therefore all the more important that your proposal does not get lost amongst all the other cold, detailed and purely factual ones of your competitors. Otherwise, the eye gets drawn to the bottom line, price; and if your price is not the best, you may lose the contract. Price is never the only buying criterion.

Who else is submitting proposals? This information is not always available but if it is, this is where S.W.O.T. (Strengths, Weaknesses, Opportunities, Threats) points can be scored.

How many people will be involved in the decision? If you can find this out along with their names it is an opportunity to present as many copies as necessary, perhaps professionally bound with smart covers, maybe with the names on the covers.

When are the proposals decided upon? Depending on how formal the meeting is, you could volunteer to be available should any amplification be needed on your proposal.

By asking yourself all the pertinent questions, you can then decide what actions you must take. But do ask all the questions. There can be a tendency to ask around your office, 'Anybody got an example of a really good proposal?'

The heaving line principle

When large ships come in to dock or when they transfer goods at sea, sailors cannot fling great four-inch manila ropes from one ship to another. Instead a nylon line is cast. A half-inch heaving line is attached to this, then perhaps a mooring spring or other heavier securing gear. The proposal should adhere broadly to this principle. Some proposals lack any finesse, readability, or any sales content. Some contain one page with just a bald fact or two. Others contain masses of data, itemising every element of the specification with model numbers, part numbers, patent numbers, pantones, dimensions and so on.

Okay, there are horses for courses, but which reads more easily:

'The XSRS1200 with QWD attachment measures 52 ins × 85 ins × 45 ins with attachment fitted (50 ins × 78 ins × 43 ins without), its overall weight is 398 kg and will be delivered in pantone 126b'

Or:

'The machine can be delivered in Autumn Grey which will blend perfectly with existing floor covering. Having checked the measurements carefully we can advise you it will fit neatly by the staffroom window. Delivery and floor loading present no problems.'

(An exact specification can be attached as an additional sheet, as in the Heaving Line Principle.)

So what comes first? You can add in or leave out what you consider necessary, but ideally a professional proposal would contain:

A Front Sheet or Cover
It contains only a few words. 'A Proposal for . . . Presented by . . .' Some front sheets contain the logo of the receiving company along with the logo of the proposing company, sometimes in colour. This can look extremely professional. If you are proposing on any form of precision equipment, this attention to detail can create a brilliant impression.

An Introductory Letter
This letter should be brief and in simple English, French or Swahili for that matter, as long as it is simple with no waffle-speak.

Dear Peter,

At our meeting on the 25th June you asked me to submit to you a proposal for a . . . You needed this for your three directors before the 5th July board meeting. To make life easier for you I have enclosed a copy for you plus one for each of your directors.

I'll call you on the 2nd July to make sure you have all the information you need.

Kind regards/Best wishes/Sincerely,
(*Depending on relationship*)

You could include that you are available to be on call on the day of the board meeting should any questions arise, but there is no need. You can do that verbally on the second of July when you call. Also you could add that if Peter has any queries in the interim period he should not hesitate to call you. But why? Presumably Peter holds a reasonably responsible position and is adequately endowed with grey matter. Quite likely too, he might resent being told the obvious. Or he may mentally respond with a sarcastic, 'Oh thank you. Actually if I have any queries I just sit here hoping someone will call me and ask if he can help'. No, keep the letter brief. Imagine what you like to read.

A Contents List
Depending on the length of the proposal this may or may not be needed.

Requirement Sheet
This sheet is a straightforward resumé of the buyer's needs. You may think this is unnecessary. It might be if only one person constituted the DMU, but if there is a committee of five people, it is important that they are all viewing the situation from exactly the same perspective.
This sheet should also be in plain English.

Your requirement was for a widget that would achieve the following:
A . . . .
B . . . .
C . . . .
D . . . .

You can add to each item the benefits the buyer obtains. Depending on circumstances you can include the short-comings of the existing system.

This would overcome the existing problems of:
A . . . .
B . . . .
C . . . .

But he knows all that! Maybe, but in some circumstances a recap can be effective in its empathy factor, not just for the recipient but for other members of the DMU who may not be fully conversant with the need. It is not uncommon to hear a member of a buying committee say, 'I didn't realise our machine didn't do . . .' or 'I had no idea we wasted so much time/material/doing . . .'

So a well presented Requirement Sheet looks professional, shows understanding and helps all the DMU to view the situation from the same perspective. As with the sales process you have established the need. Clearly the next step is prove you meet the need with a Sales Sheet:

The Package

> Having thoroughly assessed your requirements, we have no hesitation in recommending the XK1250 widget which has the capacity for:
> A . . . .
> B . . . .
> C . . . .
> D . . . .

Here you simply run over the Requirement items again and, if you wish, list the benefits to the buyer including any additional ones not covered by the Requirement Sheet. This is a good opportunity to plug your company, especially where service, support and reliability are important.

Finally you attach a *Specification Sheet* itemising dimensions, colour, accessories, model numbers and any other technical data which may be necessary.

The conclusion is price with whatever payment options there are along with any terms and conditions. This, as the cliché runs, is the bottom line. There is no need for any additional padding such as, 'We look forward . . .' or 'Awaiting your . . .' or 'Assuring you of our . . .' The introductory letter renders this superfluous.

Quotations and proposals

Most salespeople are aware of the distinction but it is worth mentioning that a quotation can form part of a binding contract. It is therefore important to make clear your conditions. The offer of goods or services should be made subject to acceptance by a fixed date after which you reserve the right to adjust the costings as necessary. Most important, it should be checked for accuracy. Numbers of payments, start dates and whether VAT is inclusive or exclusive should be shown without any ambiguity. Should you under-quote and the buyer formally accepts that quote in writing, the two documents could constitute a binding agreement in law.

A proposal, as the name suggests is less rigid and is viewed as more conditional.

Thankfully these legal niceties are mainly academic but despite a main constituent of business being trust, the commercial world can be harsh and unforgiving.

131

9

RETAIL SELLING

Years ago men who sold in shops were called salesmen and those who sold direct were known as commercial travellers or canvassers. Nowadays shop salespeople are called sales assistants. The dictionary describes an assistant as one who helps or provides assistance. Yes, you know that – pretty obvious really. Perhaps, but when one considers the standard of retail selling in the UK, one is tempted to check the dictionary in case there is a unique contrary definition for sales assistants in British editions.

We all have our views on the standard of retail sales staff, so I carried out a survey of about fifty people to establish their satisfactions and dissatisfactions. There were scarce few of the former and the latter were legion. I'll list the main ones.

Manner was probably the greatest single area. There were some excellent examples of sales staff who went to endless trouble to help a customer. Marks & Spencer merited regular praise for both manner and product knowledge – though this did vary from town to town. Comet was given several honourable mentions with regard to the product knowledge of staff in white goods and TV and hi-fi departments. These and a few others, alas, were the exceptions which proved the general rule of bad service.

Tills in supermarkets, banks and post offices have to

132

close on a regular basis for several reasons. It is not their closing but the manner in which they close that infuriates shoppers. A pleasant informative statement with an apology for inconvenience is all that is needed to achieve good customer relations. Sales staff who start bolting the doors at ten minutes to six when the hours sign clearly shows six o'clock closing, merited special wrath. Their token, 'Sorry, we're closed' made matters worse, especially as there was no real sorrow whatever in the statement – quite the reverse: there is often a note of triumph in the delivery, roughly equivalent to 'Gotcha'.

When queues form, a simple rule in retail selling is to make eye contact. Some hotels are very good at this. When four or five people are waiting to settle their bills, all a receptionist has to do to keep things calm is make eye contact with the rear person then smile and say, 'I won't keep you a moment' or words to that effect. This simple phrase can defuse a possible ugly situation.

Some effort has been made by retail managers to train their staffs. The penny has dropped that 'Can I help you?' is a closed question and will more often than not evince the answer, 'No', usually accompanied by, 'I'm just looking.' Staff are now being trained to say, 'How can I help you?'. The trouble is that many retail managers are trying to find a solution before understanding the problem. If the assistant's manner is still lifeless or sour, the combination of words really matters not a jot. As we saw in chapter 7 there is no verbal key to the sales box. It is delivery and manner which determine the reaction of the customer. Some outlets are even teaching the addition of 'please' to the question, giving us the rather unctuous, 'How can I help you please?'. Too many hotels are doing this. 'This is the Superb Hotel, Shirley speaking, how may I help you please?' – just doesn't sound right, does it? Also because of the parrot content of the phrase, the delivery often suffers.

Too many sales 'assistants' say 'Yes?' or 'Can I help you?' in a tone more befitting a householder who has just found someone trespassing in his front garden. Poor old Tracey and Sharon attracted special venom for continuing with an obviously non-business telephone call when a customer is waiting, within earshot, to be served.

This area does not indicate just a lack of sales skills; it shows an absence of common courtesy. Good manners should be a prerequisite before recruiting staff, add to that some product knowledge and sales skills, and you have the basis of a good sales assistant. Whatever happened to the simple greeting? A pleasant 'good morning' can start a sales exchange off on the right foot. Continental shopkeepers invariably greet you with 'Bonjour' or its equivalent.

Slowly the message of good service and pleasant manners is drifting across to us from the other side of the Atlantic. We still tend to snigger a little at the waitress who greets us with, 'Hi, I'm Susan. Welcome. I'll be looking after your table this evening', but we like it and it works. The restaurant chain Thank God It's Friday has adopted the warmer greeting style with more extrovert staff. The food is not exceptional but you usually have to book. Similarly the McDonalds 'Have a nice day' and 'Enjoy our meal' approach has taken the chain from nowhere to top fast food outlet in the country (and the world).

Ray Fuller, head of the Psychology Department in Trinity College, Dublin, tells me of the latest retail howler from America. Ray made a purchase in a large department store. The assistant turned to another member of staff and said, 'Would you please wrap this for our guest.' Worse was to come. When he was leaving, the lady said, 'Byee now. We're missing you already.'

However – when you have finished with the sick bag – let us not look at the content of what was said but at the intention. Granted the content is dire but the motivating force was to look after and please the customer.

We, in the UK, by rejecting the saccharine and artificial verbiage used in parts of the US, run the risk of throwing the baby out with the bathwater. Certainly these cloying phrases do not trip easily off British tongues but we should have the same determination to render the best possible service to the customer.

The introduction of an 'over 55 years of age' recruitment policy by the B&Q chain proved to be a huge success. The success seemed to merit surprise. Why? All the ingredients of success are there – better manners, more patience and interest in the customer and an all-round higher standard of knowledge acquired through a lifetime of work.

In clothes shops, ladies find it particularly galling to be followed round or told by a sales assistant, 'You'll look great in this'. Most women have a very clear idea of what they do and do not look great in. As a salesman I rather admire the positive enthusiasm of the phrase and I rejoice to see someone eager to make a sale. However, as we saw earlier, telling is not selling and the road to the salesperson's grave is paved with assumptions.

No one expects retail employers to invest in a two-week training course on sales skills and product knowledge when often staff are only temporary or part-time. However, they really should pay more attention to the very basics. As a recruitment manager for a major multinational company, my first questions are the simplest: Do I like this person? How would I feel if he or she came to make a sales presentation to me? Would I feel at ease socially with him or her? Is there warmth, a pleasant smile, good eye contact? Or more simply, how do they rate on the People Buy From People test? Granted an employer wants a few other things as well. The ability to add up and do joined-up writing helps. Intelligence, enthusiasm, eagerness to succeed and a few other more commercial qualities are essential – particularly in direct selling – but the more basic personal or human qualities must be the starting point. With this as a yardstick, how on earth do some of the unhelpful, even surly sales 'assistants' get employed?

Take that greatest of British institutions, the pub.

Tradition gives us an image of mine host, welcoming, cheerful, proud of his ale, and all-round PR man for the trade. Logically, the very function of the pub is to be place of good cheer, conviviality, warmth and bonhomie. What do we often find? Tattooed youths who cannot distinguish between natural, fresh, cask-conditioned beer and the gaseous muck of convenience products the brewers call 'keg' with its whiff of bad eggs. In Ireland, trade union influence was always very strong in the licensed trade and training played an important part in the industry. In Irish pubs you can still order a Screwdriver, a Manhattan, a Bloody Mary or an Irish coffee and be served without hesitation. Alas, in British pubs you often have to explain what you want. Just a couple of hours spent with staff in the most basic training could transform standards overnight. (We'll take a look at free houses and tenants later under the section Small is Beautiful.)

Training in sales skills, communication skills and product knowledge not only makes life pleasanter for both sides of the counter but it makes sound commercial sense. Even if an employer is a surly and greedy type who is purely interested in making money, he should invest in people skills if only to have a more successful business.

A nation of shopkeepers?

Napoleon used this phase to dismiss the English. Whatever he meant then, it hardly applies now. Why are there virtually no such things as English corner shops, restaurants or fast-food shops? Why is the French railway system the pride of France yet British Rail the butt of everyone's jokes?

This whole issue could merit a separate, lengthy study. We looked earlier at the British distaste for 'trade' and the historical bias towards the arts and away from industry. We looked at illogical class prejudice and how, for example, the US remained free from such nonsense because of a quite different development since the eighteenth century.

For whatever reasons, one thread runs through the entire customer relations issue: the British find it difficult to dissociate service from servility. The Italians, Spanish, Greeks and French, who all take machismo more seriously than we do, find no difficulty in separating service from servility. The Italians, particularly, view the restaurant business almost with a sense of theatre. The immaculate head waiter, minutely examining a spoon then clicking his fingers for some minion to take it away and replace it, is pure theatre. The fact that the minion takes the spoon into the kitchen and wipes it on the back of his trousers, is irrelevant. The staff do not compromise their dignity. They enjoy the ritual of napkins, cutlery, wine-tasting and the gloriously theatrical *pièce de résistance*, the flambé.

Also, if Wayne and Tracey are having a posh night out, the professionalism never wavers. Any uncertainty with menu or wine list is delicately glossed over. Should a customer wish to show off to his group or lady friend, fine – it's all part of the show, and if a hefty tip is flamboyantly left on the plate, so much the better.

We have difficulty with this service/servility division. Perhaps we know intellectually that you do not have to be servile to give good service, but emotionally we struggle with the distinction. In times gone by when the class barriers were much more rigid, most of our restaurants were British. We had tea shops, Lyons Corner Houses, waitresses with white pinnies, lamb chops and two veg and cake trays. Self-service was unheard of.

As the class barriers diminished, it was because we so desperately wanted to shake off the dreadful I-know-my-place servility of the past that the service/servility dilemma grew.

A parallel was found in Australia. So fiercely democratic and egalitarian were the Aussies that taxi drivers resented being given a tip. They quite reasonably felt this demeaned them and cast them in a servile role, while they saw themselves doing an honest job for an honest price and consequently could spit in anyone's eye as an equal. With the massive growth in Aussie self-confidence, these sensibilities are not now quite so delicate.

It's we Brits who have the hang-ups. We are so close to many of them that we don't notice them. A friend of mine was struck by a newsagent with a stream of customers. The newsagent said, in sequence 'Yes mate; yes mate; yes mate; yes sir; yes mate; yes sir'. No one was remotely aware of the implicit insult to all the 'mates'. The shopkeeper was making instant class decisions. Cheap anorak – yes mate. Suit, umbrella – yes sir. The observer just happened to be American and sufficiently distant from our quaint little ways to find them hilarious.

The days are dying when the second cousin of the Duke of Barchester could get a room on credit at the Ritz instantly while Herbert Grimethorpe with four grand in his hip pocket got turned away. But it's a slow death. Service is getting better. As the dreadful class barriers disappear and our self-confidence grows we are seeing service for what it is.

More British restaurants are appearing but we went through a period when virtually every restaurant was French, Italian, Chinese, Indian or of other non-British extraction. Similarly with every fast-food outlet for fish and chips, ice cream, curries or kebabs. The only good British restaurants often tended to be frightfully posh and run by people who had 'come down in the world'. They had the uncanny knack of giving the poor bourgeois punter the feeling that they were doing him a favour by serving him. They also encouraged a type of restaurant behaviour which is uniquely English. This is the extraordinary phenomenon of the class-based EROC (English Restaurant Ornithological Cry). It happens when two or more people with posh accents are seated together. They raise their voices like an ornithological hierarchical display where birds call out in the forest to let others know they are there. At a table elsewhere in the restaurant a couple of other EROC-birds might hear the cry, and not to be outdone they too display their vowel sounds. So the EROC-birds have identified each other and the restaurant staff are in no doubt who's who. The truly strange part of this phenomenon is that the other birds of less overpowering plumage actually go quiet and the real social inadequates end up whispering to each other across the table, lest the vowel sounds of their calls might betray their lowly origin. In restaurants all over the world the noise level varies from the pleasantly conversational to the cacophonous. Only in Britain can you find people whispering.

Our American brothers have never had this problem. In one bar it might be, 'What'll it be, Mac?' and in another you might hear, 'What can I get you, sir?' but the respective greetings are the same for everyone. Generally there is a desire to please the customer (so what if the motives are often purely commercial?). There is also a pride in giving the service. Even with simple food orders, you are asked how many eggs you want, how do you like them cooked, how do you want them served, what type of bread and so on. In a motorway service station in England I remember being told that the standard breakfast came with one egg. I said I wanted two and was happy to pay for two. Perhaps assuming I was mentally subnormal or hard of hearing the lady insisted breakfast meant one egg. Eventually after a little consultation I was served two. In another 'service' station I was told I could not have a mug of tea as I was not a lorry driver.

What is the problem in this country? When are we going to learn (and take as completely normal) that if a customer wants something and has the cash to pay for it, we do business. That is what trade or selling or business or commerce, call it whatever you like, is all about. I stayed for a month in one of Liverpool's top hotels. They give you a piece of paper called a key card. Breakfast is not inclusive so you are supposed to show your key card to assist assigning the cost of your meal to your bill. One morning I was in a hurry. The 'assistant' knew my name. I had been there three weeks. I had my room key with me. My room number had not changed. Yet I could not have breakfast without my key card. I fetched the duty manager who saw sense, but the damage was done. I checked out at the end of the week and moved to another hotel. When the system becomes more important than the customer for whom the system should be designed, you have lost your objective.

The death of the British-run corner shop was self-inflicted. Cake shops sold cakes, paper shops sold papers and food shops sold food. 'We don't sell eggs' or 'We don't sell shoelaces' was a reply delivered with the finality of words carved in stone. Our Asian brothers had no such reservations. Before the second request for an item, Mr Patel had them in stock.

Banks would open once you were in your place of work, they would close when you went to lunch, open again when you were back in the office and close again at 3.30. Post offices and many retail outlets would have fewer instead of more staff serving at lunch time, when they were needed most.

The British concept of business was rather like a pyramid of importance. The chairman was on top, then the board of directors, then middle managers, junior managers, secretarial staff, workers, sales staff and finally the customer. A customer who wished to speak to the chairman would be told that the chairman was too important. Yet it is the customer who pays everyone's wages. The Americans tended to invert the pyramid of importance with the customer on top and salespeople second. It is told of Walt Disney that when he could not be found for important board meetings, he was often traced to the Disneyland car park talking to the staff. Disney was anxious about the morale and general attitude of the car parking staff. He reasoned that they were the first contact his Disneyland customers had. If the staff were courteous, helpful and cheerful, the mood of the customers and their entire disposition to Disneyland would be favourable. They would enjoy their day more, spend more and tell more of their friends. The board meeting could wait. The car park was the coal face.

We're learning. Banks are more flexible. Shops are taking on extra part-time staff for peak periods. Supermarkets are open all hours. Service stations are selling more goods than ever before, including milk, fruit, flowers, cassettes and souvenirs. Pubs are now serving some of the best food in the country where once the landlord's imagination failed beyond a pork pie, a pickled egg or ploughman's lunch. Cinemas are offering up to a dozen movie choices, providing food and drink and accepting credit cards. The customer is slowly fighting his way to his rightful position at the top of the pyramid of importance.

Small is beautiful

The fundamental principle that the customer is king has taken a long time to percolate through the corporate mind. Rationalisation, standardisation and progress were the weasel words of the Big is Beautiful trend in the Sixties and Seventies. The objective was to suit the manufacturer or supplier. Bread became standard white, characterless and low in nutrition. Sausages were mass-produced, anaemic and flavourless. The wonderful variety of scrumptious British apples diminished to the monotonous Golden Delicious and one or two others.

Natural cask-conditioned beer had been produced by thousands of breweries with an infinite combination of flavours, strengths, colours hopping-rates and head densities. Wonderful for the customer and the pride of

Britain. Not so for the suppliers. Because the beers were natural and organic they could 'go off'. Delivery needed care. Looking after them needed time, knowledge and training. With the Big is Beautiful movement the smaller brewers were taken over one by one.

Up to the sixties, no man ever drank lager. It was a lady's drink. Men drinking lager were looked upon with suspicion and a man drinking lager and lime was tantamount to 'coming out'. But the brewers wanted standardisation, convenience and more profit. Their ad men put on the television macho images of men toiling on oil rigs or coming off a rugby pitch. They gave their lagers big butch names like Charger and Norseman. Slowly the younger drinkers capitulated to the point where many bars were awash with uniform, crystal-clear, inorganic, fizzy convenience products. The lager could be delivered in tankers, any distance at any temperature. The brewers and the landlords were happy. Britain's glorious heritage of natural beers all but disappeared in some areas. Hand pumps were ripped out and the bright, illuminated fonts of progress were installed everywhere.

Perhaps the greatest casualty to standardisation was the British high street. Whereas in the past every high street had its local shop names, each one boasting its individuality, now with chain stores and franchises, every high street from Aberdeen to Penzance looks the same. But the customer is fighting back. Bakers now have to make traditional wholewheat bread in many varieties. The customer will not accept white cotton wool. Butchers are producing sausages with flavour. Real beer is back in the pubs and hand pumps no longer merit surprise. There are still far too few free houses with proud and knowledgeable staff but the convenience of the supplier is at last becoming secondary to the convenience of the customer.

Manners maketh sales

No matter what formulae or marketing concepts we employ, the sales transaction is between two people. To succeed in retail selling, it is essential to recruit and train the right people. The restaurant or pub with a friendly atmosphere and good service will always do better business than one with trendy decor or an ultra-modern theme.

Many shoppers complain of the manner of staff when faulty goods have to be returned. Some stores do have a 'no quibble' policy; if the customer is not happy they do not even ask why, a full refund is given on request. But far too often the 'assistant's' reaction is one of tired resignation and what a nuisance it all is. This is a shockingly shortsighted attitude. If anyone should feel annoyed, it has to be the customer. If the retailer wishes to secure good customer relations and future sales the unhappy buyer should be treated with extra attention, not less.

Today's pattern is to make retail selling less and less labour intensive. Attractively displayed goods and self-service are now the norm. This might influence retailers to concentrate less on recruitment and staff training. The logic of this is unclear. Surely with fewer staff the attention to recruitment and training should be greater.

In the previous chapters on direct selling, we examined how we sell four things: yourself, your product, your company, your price. The Yourself element will never be as strong in retail sales because of the very professional marketing, presentation and pricing techniques which have been developed. However, there is a danger in believing that because the You element is less important it might also be unimportant.

The You factor is still pre-eminent in many cases. Who does not have a favourite hairdresser, shoe-repairer, plumber or butcher? Pub landlords who remember customers' names and what they drink retain more regulars than the trendier wine bars which flourish and die like mushrooms. Who minds an extra few pounds when the restaurant proprietor greets us and makes a fuss of us?

Some manuals on successful selling talk of the three A s – Ability, Activity, Attitude. In retail selling, you'll hear the same complaints about the first two, but the most damning by far is, 'I just didn't like his attitude'.

10

ATTITUDE

The final words must be on attitude. In an exercise I conduct with salespeople, I tell them they are all promoted to sales managers. Before the promotion can be effected, they have to recruit a replacement for themselves. I ask them to list all the qualities they would seek in a successful salesperson. Then I draw a line down a flip-chart writing some of the qualities they choose on one side and some on the other.

One side is invariably four or five times longer than the other. The long side includes such factors as enthusiasm, punctuality, confidence, perseverance, hardwork, good humour, the will to win, being success-oriented and several others. The short side is sometimes blank or contains only one or two qualities of a different nature. What divides the two columns? Without knowing the purpose of the exercise the salesmen choose attitude-related qualities as by far the more important. The ability or skill factors are rated a poor second.

In that brief exercise we are unanimously agreed that attitude is the bedrock of success. If it needed any more proof it is worth dwelling on the awe-inspiring numbers of men and women who have striven against insuperable odds to succeed. In Christy Brown's autobiography *My Left Foot* we see a man who achieves fame as a writer and artist, yet can only communicate through writing with his eponymous limb.

The number of women who have fought against male-dominated institutions to achieve greatness is a testament to attitude first, ability second. Attitude can take football teams, athletes, invalids, entrepreneurs and salespeople from the mediocre to the excellent.

On your way home from a restaurant you realise you left your wallet containing only a few pounds behind. You return and find the premises locked up. What do you do? You probably go home and call in the morning. But say there was a £50 note in the wallet? You'd probably ring the bell, maybe leave a note under the door and call first thing in the morning. What if you'd left a carry-cot with your baby under the table, and you saw flames coming from the kitchen. Is access a problem? None whatever. Would the door be smashed open in one minute flat? Of course it would. Same restaurant, same door. What changed? Your *attitude*.

You need £10,000 for a super holiday next year. Can you earn it? Maybe. Maybe not. You need £10,000 for a life-saving operation for you or someone you love. Can you raise it?

Perhaps the situations are over dramatised but the point is proved.

Selling is the most equal profession of all. We all start with exactly the same amount of the key commodity – time. How we use it is conditioned by attitude. Either sit at a desk and complain about your manager, your area, the weather, the economic climate, or set yourself written daily, weekly and monthly goals. It is up to you. If you genuinely believe your product or company is not good enough, leave it, go and sell something else. My golden rule in life is:

NEVER COMPLAIN ABOUT A SITUATION YOU HAVE THE
POWER TO CHANGE

Ability helps but attitude determines success. Look at the TV quiz show, *Mastermind*. Contestant after contestant with brains to burn. Ranges of knowledge that are ency-clopedic. Yet look at the jobs – librarian, school teacher, civil servant, taxi driver and a sprinkling of the unemployed and the retired.

Most limitations are self-imposed. Negative people are really rather stupid. They'll find half a dozen reasons why they cannot achieve something, but they only need one.

Place a sticker above your bathroom mirror which reads, *'The buck stops with you'*. In a perfect world we would receive a series of lucky breaks but in this world you make your own luck.

Despite that, I wish you lots of it.

INDEX